The No-Fault Classroom

Tools to Resolve Conflict & Foster Relationship Intelligence

Sura Hart and Victoria Kindle Hodson

PuddleDancer
P R E S S

P.O. Box 231129, Encinitas, CA 92023-1129
email@PuddleDancer.com ▪ www.PuddleDancer.com

The No-Fault Classroom:
Tools to Resolve Conflict & Foster Relationship Intelligence

© 2008 Sura Hart and Victoria Kindle Hodson
A PuddleDancer Press Book

PuddleDancer Press, Permissions Dept.
P.O. Box 231129, Encinitas, CA 92023-1129
Fax: 858-759-6967, email@PuddleDancer.com

Authors: Sura Hart and Victoria Kindle Hodson
Illustrators: Anita Griffin (Twin characters and elements)
and Martin Mellein, MGM Graphic Design
(Feelings and Needs characters and elements; Giraffe Note of Appreciation)
Index: Phyllis Linn, INDEXPRESS
Book Design: Lightbourne, Inc.

Manufactured in the United States of America

1st Printing, August 2008

10 9 8 7 6 5 4 3 2 1

ISBN: 978-1-892005-18-2

Library of Congress Cataloging-in-Publication Data

Hart, Sura.
   The no-fault classroom : tools to resolve conflict & foster relationship intelligence / Sura Hart and Victoria Kindle Hodson.
       p. cm.
   Includes bibliographical references and index.
   ISBN 978-1-892005-18-2 (softcover : alk. paper)
1. Classroom management.   2. Teacher-student relationships.   3. Effective teaching.
I. Kindle Hodson, Victoria.   II. Title.

LB3013.H3573 2008
372.1102'4--dc22

                              2008027943

Support for *The No-Fault Classroom*

"The brilliant, 'no-fault classroom' concept could create a cultural tsunami, revolutionizing the comparison-based identity culture of our schools today. A must read for all educators!"

—STEPHEN R. COVEY, author, *The 7 Habits of Highly Effective People*
and *The 8th Habit: From Effectiveness to Greatness*

"Years of hard work, practice, practical insight and mastery are packed into every page. Sura and Victoria will take you by the hand, open your heart and transform your classroom. I can't recommend this clear and passionate practice highly enough."

—MICHAEL MENDIZZA, author and founder, Touch the Future

"*The No-Fault Classroom* brings history alive as my students and I explore the universal needs that people are trying to meet."

—DEB PIEROTTI, 3rd–4th grade teacher

To our teachers, who shared with us their fervor
for developing the capacities of the heart
as well as the mind.

◉   ◉   ◉

To our students, of all ages and in many parts of the world,
who practice Nonviolent Communication in
their families, schools and communities.

Contents

Appendices

Acknowledgements

We are grateful to the late Caroline Hawley, healer of souls and dear friend, who first introduced us to Nonviolent Communication;

to Marshall B. Rosenberg, international peacemaker and founder of Nonviolent Communication, who brings us inspiration and hope for a more peaceful and sustainable world;

to Kyra Freestar, our editor, who contributed her skills with language and structure, connected with our message and created a fun, productive, collaborative writing partnership;

to family and friends who continually support us in our work, and especially to Stan Hodson, who cooks for us and cheers us on, holds a big vision for our work and so willingly shares his expertise;

and to our children, Brian, Kyra and Marieka, who open our hearts and minds to the wonder and necessity of Inner Space exploration.

Introduction

If educators are serious about reducing the conflict and emotional stress that limit the amount and quality of learning taking place in classrooms, then it is time to provide teachers and students with the skills they need to create safe, co-operative learning environments.

Increased self-knowledge and improved communication skills result in fewer conflicts, more co-operation, and a dramatic increase in the time students spend in engaged learning. *The No-Fault Classroom: Tools to Resolve Conflict & Foster Relationship Intelligence* provides teachers and students with these skills.

The *No-Fault Classroom* Approach to Conflict Prevention & Resolution

Whether you want a respectful, peaceful classroom and school and see the classroom microcosm as a model and training ground for a peaceful and sustainable world, or you want a classroom and school where students feel safe enough to give their attention and the full stretch of their minds and hearts to learning and discovery, or you want all of the above, this curriculum provides the tools.

The link between engaged learning and students' needs for physical and emotional safety in classrooms has been clearly established. The work of Maria Montessori, Paul MacLean, William Glasser, John Holt, Joseph Chilton Pearce, Nel Noddings, Daniel Siegel, Allan N. Schore, Alfie Kohn and Daniel Goleman, among many others, has converged in the last decade to contribute to an understanding that emotionally stressful environments threaten children's sense of safety and well-being and are not conducive to learning. While this news from the fields of brain science, psychology, medicine and education continues to come in, the news from distressed teachers is of increases in student discontent, resistance and conflict in the classroom—all symptoms of fear, stress and lack of emotional safety.

Shootings in schools, as well as rising rates of preteen and teen suicide, are poignant and tragic indicators that tell us young people have been under great emotional stress for a long time.

Establishing lasting peace is the work of education; all politics can do is keep us out of war.

—Maria Montessori

A significant cause of the increasing stress in students (and also in teachers) is the decades-long choice of school officials to encourage and fund classroom discipline and management programs rather than communication skills and self-development programs.

Strategies to manage student behavior have repeatedly trumped programs that develop Relationship Intelligence. Instead of focusing on monitoring, punishing and rewarding students, programs designed to foster Relationship Intelligence help teachers develop skills to build relationships with students and to identify students' needs and help them find ways to meet them. Teachers also provide forums where students can voice their concerns and learn how to listen and express themselves clearly.

We believe that the high level of anxiety and stress that teachers (and parents) are seeing in young people is a sign that time has run out for managerial discipline programs, and the time for developing the human capacity for Relationship Intelligence has arrived. The high costs of current policies, including truancy, detentions, suspensions, dropout numbers and failure to graduate from high school are becoming more obvious by the day. We have the means to develop students' capacities to take more responsibility for their learning; identify and find ways to meet their own needs; identify and help others fulfill their needs; communicate honestly and effectively; and have a constructive voice in policies, practices and decisions that affect them. What we need now is the will and commitment to bring these capacities to reality. It is our belief that when developing Relationship Intelligence replaces managing behavior in classrooms across the country, and is complemented by various differentiated instruction practices, we will see a drop in student discontent, resistance and conflict in classrooms and an unprecedented increase in engaged, eager learning.

Experiments in creating relationship-based classrooms and schools that address the needs of all members of a learning community have been under way for several decades; in the last few years they have dramatically increased in numbers, as stresses in the traditional system reach a breaking point. We are encouraged to see more educators insist on tending to the real needs of their students instead of spending their time teaching to standardized tests and enforcing policies that are clearly failing to create the safe, respectful, high-quality schools everyone wants. Physical safety, emotional safety and a sense of well-being are foundational needs that, when met, allow students to turn their attention to and fully engage their minds in the pursuit of learning—which is after all, under supportive conditions, what humans naturally love to do.

Our earlier book *The Compassionate Classroom: Relationship Based Teaching and Learning* was written to introduce teachers to the Nonviolent Communication process originally developed by Marshall Rosenberg, PhD,

> We should want more from our educational efforts than adequate academic achievement, and we will not achieve even that meager success unless our children believe that they themselves are cared for and learn to care for others.
>
> —Nel Noddings

It also lays a foundation for applying the premises of Nonviolent Communication to the classroom. We began writing *The No-Fault Classroom* in response to teachers' subsequent requests for day-by-day and step-by-step lesson plans that develop the premises and valuable communication skills introduced in *The Compassionate Classroom*.

This present book is designed as a guide and manual for your do-it-together construction of a No-Fault Classroom. *This curriculum goes well beyond simply teaching students a conflict resolution process.* Its objective is to create the conditions in your classroom that will result in students' genuine interest and ability to care for the well-being of everyone, and a learning community built on mutual respect and willing co-operation. At the same time, students will develop powerful skills for effective problem solving and conflict resolving—skills which will result in a dramatic decrease in the number of conflicts.

If a vision of the substantive and far-reaching results of fostering Relationship Intelligence by constructing a No-Fault Classroom inspires you, we hope you will also appreciate that this curriculum requires a commitment on the teacher's part: to carefully prepare the ground, lay the foundation and guide the construction efforts of your class. We hope the brief introduction to the curriculum that follows (as well as a look through the introductory sections, materials list and classroom modules) will serve to inform you of what is involved.

The No-Fault Classroom Curriculum

The *No-Fault Classroom* curriculum is organized into three sections:

Section I – Prepare the Ground & Lay the Foundation
Section II – Construction Materials
Section III – Construct Your No-Fault Classroom

Section I – Prepare the Ground & Lay the Foundation

Prepare the Ground: Teacher Exploration. We invite teachers to prepare themselves to work with the primary themes of the curriculum by doing several exercises. The Teacher Explorations in Section I include explorations of conflict, its causes and its effects on learning; how teachers use their power and engage co-operation in the classroom; and the underlying intention that motivates teachers' actions in the classroom.

Lay the Foundation: Class Meetings. Teachers are asked to call two class meetings to lay a firm foundation of safety and trust prior to the introduction of the *No-Fault Classroom* curriculum. In the first Class Meeting, teachers are asked to share with students the kind of classroom they would like to create and find out from students the kind of classroom they would like to participate in and contribute to. Together teacher and students come up with a group Vision that is inclusive, inspiring and motivating.

In the second Class Meeting, teachers facilitate a discussion about what makes a community physically and emotionally safe so that learning can take place. Out of this discussion, the class generates Group Agreements that meet everyone's needs for safety, trust, respect and learning. The Group Agreements are not a static set of rules, but a living contract that is referred to, discussed and revised as needed throughout the year.

Section II – Construction Materials

The No-Fault Classroom is a material-rich curriculum. During the 18 modules, students will create a set of materials that they will use throughout the school year. An overview of the templates, blueprints and directions for making materials is found in Section II.

The primary materials are the Internal Operating System (IOS) Power Panel and three Card Decks. The IOS Power Panel provides visual clarity for a complex internal realm. The Card Decks familiarize students with the many needs and feelings that exist in their IOS and acquaint them with the choices they have in every situation. By working with the Power Panel and Card Decks, students, in conflict and non-conflict situations, determine which area of their IOS needs attention, what choices they have and what choice they want to make.

All members of the classroom can get a visual picture of others' IOSs also, by changing places with each other and looking at the Cards each has placed on their Power Panels. This is a powerful way to see the needs at the root of conflicts. The topic of conversation then turns to finding ways to meet needs, rather than to who is right and who is wrong.

Altogether, these tools will support and maintain your No-Fault Classroom for the entire school year, so we suggest you consider carefully how you want to set up and conduct material construction for the most ease and enjoyment.

Please look at Section II for a more detailed outline of this important aspect of the *No-Fault Classroom* curriculum and a list of secondary materials to be used for construction and for classroom signs and messages.

Section III – Construct Your No-Fault Classroom

The *No-Fault Classroom* curriculum comprises twenty-one class sessions of approximately one hour each. The first two sessions are the Class Meetings discussed in Section I, in which you and your students will develop a Classroom Vision and Group Agreements for establishing safety and trust. An Introduction to the No-Fault Zone directs students to construct one of the primary tools for the curriculum, the IOS Power Panel. The remaining 18 classroom modules are organized in pairs to explore 9 human Powers (discussed in more detail below).

We developed this curriculum with the idea that it would be presented over approximately eleven weeks at the beginning of the school year, with the two Class Meetings and Introduction to the No-Fault Zone held during the first two weeks, and the 18 modules following at a rate of approximately two modules per week. When a class has completed the *No-Fault Classroom* curriculum, students and teacher alike will have gained skills they can practice and use during the remainder of the year and beyond—skills to communicate effectively, avert conflict and resolve conflict peacefully.

Introduction to the No-Fault Zone

The Introduction to the No-Fault Zone is a one-hour, hands-on activity during which students make one of the primary tools they will be using: their Internal Operating System Power Panel. They are also introduced to their guides for this inward-bound journey, Nao and Michi—sixteen-year-old twin brother and sister who reside in a dimension called the No-Fault Zone.

In this session and in each of the 18 modules of the curriculum that follow, the Twins share information about the No-Fault Zone. They also provide step-by-step activities in which students explore and learn to navigate the dynamic depths of the human Internal Operating System (IOS)—a network of subtle, often unexamined and undeveloped capacities that we call the 9 Powers. These Powers relate to thoughts, feelings, needs, observations and decision-making. The goal and challenge of the curriculum is to activate these capacities and expand the range of choices teachers and students have to communicate effectively, to avert conflict and to resolve conflict peacefully. As teacher and students work through the curriculum together, they are empowered to make choices that contribute to their own well-being as well as the well-being of others.

These are the human capacities, or Powers, developed in this curriculum:

1. The Power to Get to Calm Alert

2. The Power to Know What You Need

We can't change the whole world alone, but if I can teach people that if you put your hand in mine and little by little we join more hands … maybe we can construct a new world.

—Farliz Calle, at 15, a leader in the Children's Peace Movement in Colombia nominated for the 1998 Nobel Peace Prize

3. The Power to Find Ways to Meet Needs

4. The Power to Read Feelings

5. The Power to Observe

6. The Power to Listen

7. The Power to Navigate the Fault Zone

8. The Power to Co-operate to Solve Problems & Conflicts

9. The Power to Create a No-Fault Zone Wherever You Are

Explorations: The 9 Powers in 18 Modules

Each of the 18 modules takes approximately 60 minutes to complete. In each module, the Twins provide a Narrative (Notes from the No-Fault Zone), a list of Facts and a Message. This information introduces the concept for the module and establishes a context for it. Students volunteer to take turns reading the Narratives, Facts and Messages. The step-by-step guidance the Twins provide shows teacher and students how to access, understand and develop the 9 basic human Powers.

In addition to the Twins' Narratives, Facts and Messages, each module includes activities in which teacher and students together explore the Powers of their Internal Operating System (IOS) and practice the skills that develop the Powers. The activities involve reading, writing, discussing, drawing, role-playing and constructing materials.

The activities for each module include the following:

Explorations: Students and teacher are given directions for conducting an exploration of each concept and practicing the skills introduced in the module.

Supporting Activities: These are short activities to support skill development for the current module and review and practice skills introduced in previous modules. The supporting activities can be introduced throughout the week.

Follow-on Explorations: In some modules, optional activities that support additional skill development and learning are provided, and teachers may choose to make time for these during the week.

Curricular Tie-ins: These are suggestions for ways to apply the specific concepts and skills introduced in each module to other subject areas.

This curriculum supports your literature, history and social studies curricula. As students activate and practice each of the Powers, they can start

> When we understand the needs that motivate our own and others' behavior, we have no enemies.
>
> —Marshall B. Rosenberg

applying their new awareness to other classroom studies. They will develop insight into the feelings, needs, thoughts and motivations of characters in literature as well as figures in history. Their eyes will be opened to the causes of interpersonal conflicts that provide dramatic focus in most literature as well as for historical and current conflicts between groups and between nations. As a result, these subjects will come alive in new and engaging ways.

This curriculum contributes to your science curriculum. The Twins invite teachers and students, as they embark on this inward-bound journey, to set aside preconceived ideas and take part in a laboratory-like exploration. Students and teachers are asked to experiment, wonder, observe, record results and critically evaluate what they experience and learn.

This curriculum supports your reading program. Each module provides students with scripts to read that introduce new concepts. Additionally, student volunteers take turns acting out the Twins' Narratives for each module. (Teachers are invited to read the teacher's scripts as they are written or to put them in their own language if that is more meaningful and fun.)

Above all, the Twins hope the journey is enjoyable for everyone and they encourage teachers to facilitate the Explorations in a way that optimizes fun along with learning that reaches across all subject areas.

What It Takes to Explore Inner Space

This curriculum is designed for teacher and students to explore together the inner dimensions of the Internal Operating System, with support from the Twins, the guided Explorations and the materials. Teachers are asked to be co-explorers, not experts. Teachers do not need to have prior knowledge of the 9 Powers—the communication skills and strategies taught in the curriculum. However, we expect the best results when teachers have the following in mind:

- willingness to suspend preconceived ideas

- desire to check things out for oneself (and not simply dismiss or believe what the Twins say)

- observation skills (which will be developed throughout the modules, and especially in Power 5: The Power to Observe)

- curiosity (which we also expect to develop and grow as the modules progress)

Constructing a No-Fault Classroom, similar to other worthwhile endeavors, requires commitment, careful preparation, and enthused and sustained effort. We predict that if you choose to commit to this curriculum, you will be overjoyed with the classroom environment you and your students co-create.

> Conflict skills can be powerful tools for positive liberty, with which students become more able to solve their own problems and to express their interests in ways that can be effectively heard.
>
> —Kathy Bickmore

We also expect and hope that you will find lots of fun and learning as you and your students explore the 9 Powers of the human Internal Operating System (IOS). We believe that the dimensions of Inner Space exploration are as fathomless as those of Outer Space. And we feel confident that those who are willing to embark on this inward-bound journey will discover or renew many capacities that will contribute not only to a thriving classroom but also to a more peaceful and sustainable world.

We hope you will neither simply dismiss this claim nor simply believe it, but that you will, along with your students, explore with eyes, heart and mind wide open.

Enjoy the journey!

Charting Progress

For teachers who are interested in determining the effects of the curriculum on student interactions, co-operation and participation, an **Observation Survey** is provided in **Appendix 1**. This survey can be used to establish a baseline of behaviors prior to starting the program and to chart progress at four- to six-week intervals throughout the curriculum.

Section I

Prepare the Ground & Lay the Foundation

We hope you, and your students, will enjoy planning and constructing your No-Fault Classroom throughout the school year. Your joint explorations and the structure you create together have the potential to support a learning environment that works for everyone. The time you take at the beginning to prepare the ground for the foundation of your structure will be time well spent.

To prepare the ground and lay a firm foundation for your No-Fault Classroom, we strongly encourage you to take time, before starting the modules, to do the following:

- ☐ Examine your current beliefs about conflict.
- ☐ Look at your classroom management style and its underlying assumptions about how you use power.
- ☐ Create your Vision for your classroom.
- ☐ Share your Vision with your students and hear their Visions.
- ☐ Co-create Classroom Group Agreements with your students.

> Power is of two kinds. One is obtained by fear of punishment, and the other by acts of love. Power based on love is a thousand times more effective and permanent than the one derived from fear of punishment.
>
> —Mahatma Gandhi

Prepare the Ground for Your No-Fault Classroom

To begin, we invite you to examine some of your present thinking about power, conflict and classroom management to see what assumptions and understandings you are taking into this exploration with your students.

Reflection on Conflict

Please use the guidelines below during some relaxed time to think about what conflict means to you; the causes of conflict and its effects on learning; and your current thoughts about how to prevent, reduce and resolve conflict.

After you reflect on these questions, we will share with you our own responses to the same questions.

Teacher Exploration:

Your Understanding of Conflict, Its Causes, Its Effects & What Prevents, Reduces and Resolves It

What is conflict?

Punishment damages goodwill and self-esteem, and shifts our attention from the intrinsic value of an action to external consequences.

—Marshall B. Rosenberg

_____

_____

_____

_____

_____

_____

_____

What are the causes of conflict?

_____

_____

_____

_____

_____

_____

_____

_____

How does conflict affect classroom learning?

_____

_____

_____

_____

_____

_____

_____

_____

What prevents, reduces and resolves conflict?

_____

_____

_____

_____

_____

_____

_____

_____

Our Understanding of Conflict, Its Causes, Its Effects & What Prevents, Reduces and Resolves It

What is conflict?

We begin with Webster's dictionary definition of *conflict*: "competitive or opposing action resulting from [a perception of] opposing needs, drives or wishes."

The *con-* in conflict is equivalent to *com-*, which means together; the root, *fligare*, means "to strike." In short, conflict is "striking together," as in a fight, battle or war.

Simple situations can be either relatively minor problems to be solved or the start of a fight. Trish hits Alfredo. Yukiko grabs Ryan's pencil and won't give it back. Jenny didn't turn in her homework for the third time this week. What determines, in each of these cases, whether an argument or fight will ensue?

From a behavioral point of view, if any of the players in the above inter-changes uses criticism, blame or name-calling, the scales tip in favor of conflict. Each exchange of blaming actions and words contributes to flaring tempers and moves Trish and Alfredo, Yukiko and Ryan, and Jenny and the teacher closer to the battle zone.

In conflict situations, name-calling, hitting, criticism and blame are often all that teachers and administrators see and hear before assigning blame themselves and handing out punishments. Conflict, however, is a more complex dynamic with much deeper roots. Those who are willing to ask why students call each other names, hit each other, and criticize and blame one another can discover the true nature of conflict and be primed to find new, creative ways to get to the roots of it and work with it rather than manage or suppress it.

What are the causes of conflict?

Again, taking off from Webster's definition: *conflict* is "competitive or opposing action resulting from [the perception of] opposing needs, drives or wishes."

If we're in a situation where we think that our needs, drives or wishes won't be considered or can't be met, we perceive danger and feel afraid. This is an automatic response. We're not in control of it. Our whole physiology shifts to protecting ourselves. Stress hormones are released that shut down the reasoning zones of the brain. Simplified, binary, either/or, black-and-white thinking takes over: I'm right, you're wrong. You're to blame. In short order, "you" become "the enemy."

Fight, Flight, Freeze

When we are in danger, perceived or actual, we respond automatically with a fight, flight or freeze reaction: we lash out (hit, scream, blame others) OR try to escape the situation (lie, blame ourselves, run away), OR freeze in our tracks (cower, cry, shake). Any of these reactions is likely to set off a chain reaction of judgmental, punitive responses from those around us, who are often equally stressed. The situation escalates and the understanding and reasoned response that can lead to resolution is deferred.

When conflict is dealt with in our habitual ways—by finding out who is to blame and punishing that person—fear and resentment are left smoldering, and conflict will soon flare up again.

As we see it, the root of this conflict, and all conflict, is *the thought or perception that my needs aren't going to get met in this situation.* The fear generated by this thought triggers a protective, defensive reaction that sets the conflict in motion and keeps it fueled.

How does conflict affect classroom learning?

Emotional safety is a fundamental requirement for learning. Under the emotional stress of conflict, the learning zones of the brain shut down. It is not possible, in the midst of a stressful, fearful thought, to focus one's attention on tasks that require reason, concentration, creativity or timetables for completion.

What prevents, reduces and resolves conflict?

To prevent, reduce and resolve conflict, we need to create learning communities where all students and teachers are assured that their needs matter and can be met. If we are certain that our needs do matter and that there will be an attempt to understand and address them, we are not likely to perceive danger and go into a fear response. We will have no reason to take a protective or defensive stance.

As well as assurance that everyone's needs matter equally, each member of the learning community will need a thorough knowledge of their inner landscape—thoughts, feelings, needs and choices—so they can sort through complex emotions, recognize their needs, express them clearly, strategize ways to meet them and help others do the same. In learning communities like this, problem solving is more common than conflict. And conflict can be addressed and worked through with everyone's needs in mind.

> We see things the way our minds have instructed our eyes to see.
>
> —Muhammad Yunus, founder of Grameen Bank and 2006 Nobel Peace Prize winner

Reflection on Classroom Management Style

Part of preparing the ground to construct a No-Fault Classroom is taking stock of your current reality—your policies and practices for conducting your classroom. We offer here some of the classroom management styles we have seen used by teachers.

The *authoritarian management style* values rules, respect for authority and obedience. The behaviors of those who don't comply with these expectations are suppressed with threats, incentives, rewards, consequences and punishment. Administrators and teachers determine positive and negative re-enforcers. Commands and demands are common. Students learn to obey because they fear what will happen if they don't. Students' needs are not recognized. Results: Lack of respect, resistance, withdrawal, rebelliousness and conflict are daily occurrences in these classrooms.

The *permissive management style*, which often appears in reaction to authoritarian structures and policies, prioritizes meeting student needs for free expression and choice. Teachers often understate their own needs when using a permissive management style. Eventually, when students are "out of control" and teachers are exhausted, the pendulum swings back and teachers resort to an authoritarian management style to restore order and balance. Results: This style creates an oscillating management structure that often results in confusion (for both teacher and students), resistance, lack of respect and dependency.

The *authoritative management style* provides students some choices within a clear and firm structure. Teachers guide and facilitate learning. Teachers show students the path to achieve outcomes, and students learn that they have control over some outcomes. The authoritative style values consistency, a high level of performance, firm adult expectations, consistent and firm adult-created policies and consequences, and opportunities offered to students to learn independence. Administrators and teachers remain in primary control of expectations and rules, incentives and consequences. Some needs of students are addressed and some are not. Results: A softer tone is achieved than with the authoritative style, though behavior is still managed through external "incentives" and "consequences." Students who meet expected performance standards thrive.

A *relationship-based management style* values the needs of students and teachers in the classroom equally and tries to find ways to understand and address them. Mutual decision making and mutual objective setting are learned and practiced. A relationship-based process for dialogue is taught and

> Peace cannot be kept by force. It can only be achieved by understanding.
>
> —Albert Einstein

Classroom Management Styles:

Authoritarian	Permissive	Authoritative	Relationship-based
Values rules, respect for authority, obedience	Values students' needs for free expression & choice	Values high performance, consistency, structure, student choice	Values teacher's & students' needs equally
Teacher makes rules	Students make rules	Teacher makes rules	Mutual objective setting
Teacher makes decisions	Students make decisions	Teacher makes decisions	Mutual decision making
Commands & demands Punitive use of force	Dialogue & demands Oscillates between punitive and protective use of force	Dialogue & expectations Mild punitive enforcement	Relationship-based dialogue Protective use of force only
Fosters fear of imposed punitive discipline	Offers freedom with little or no discipline	Supports looking outside oneself for discipline	Fosters self-confidence and self-discipline

used to engage co-operation. Students want to co-operate because they see that their contributions are valued. Force is employed only to protect what members of the learning community value. There is no judgment, blame or punishment for those whose behavior is not supporting the agreed-upon values; instead, there is an intent to identify and address the needs behind the behavior. Results: Mutual respect, caring, genuine co-operation and the ability to focus on learning tasks.

The *No-Fault Classroom* curriculum guides teachers in gradually developing a more and more relationship-based management style in their classroom.

Two Ways to Use Power in the Classroom

Underlying each of the management styles is one of two ways to use power: *power over* others, most fully represented by the authoritarian management style; and *power with* others, most fully represented by the relationship-based management style.

Teachers' moment-by-moment interactions with students are based on either exercising power over them or power with them. Check the following *power over* expressions and *power with* expressions that you most frequently hear yourself using.

Power Over Expressions

- ☐ *You must do this right now! If you don't…*
- ☐ *Don't make me ask you again!*
- ☐ *You are expected to do what you're told.*
- ☐ *I know that this isn't interesting or important to you, but you have to* _____.
- ☐ *How many times must I repeat myself?*
- ☐ *If you talk disrespectfully to me you will be sent to the office.*

Do you find yourself:

- ☐ lecturing?
- ☐ advising?
- ☐ arguing?
- ☐ analyzing?

Do you hear yourself:

☐ making commands?

☐ making demands?

Do you hear yourself using these or similar phrases:

☐ *you have to*

☐ *you must*

☐ *you ought to*

☐ *you should*

Power With Expressions

☐ *I'd like to find a solution that works for everyone.*

☐ *I'm happy when we work together.*

☐ *I'd like to hear how this sounds to you.*

☐ *I wonder what you need right now.*

☐ *Would you be willing to _____?*

☐ *Please help me understand what you have in mind.*

☐ *I wonder what comes up for you hearing what I said?*

☐ *I'd like to tell you what isn't working for me about this situation.*

☐ *I'd like to tell you what is working for me about this situation.*

In conflict situations, as in all other situations, the primary message of a teacher with a relationship-based style of management is this:

☐ *I want us to come up with strategies and solutions that work for all of us.*

☐ *I'm willing to explore with you ways to do that.*

Teachers determined to exercise *power with* their students are not afraid to listen to what students have to say. In fact, they welcome it. Listening doesn't mean agreeing or disagreeing. Listening is often the beginning of a dialogue that has the potential to get to the real root of problems and conflicts.

> There are three ways of dealing with difference: domination, compromise and integration. By domination only one side gets what it wants; by compromise neither side gets what it wants; by integration we find a way by which both sides may get what they wish.
>
> —Mary Parker Follett

Whether you are building on a *power over* or a *power with* foundation, your students will be learning how to address problems and conflicts from everything you say and do. They will pick up your tactics and use them with their classmates and friends. They will take your tactics home with them as a foundation for interactions with siblings, and they will use them to build a foundation for future relationships.

Power With = True Co-operation

We hear how much teachers want co-operation in their classrooms; in many cases, how desperate they are for it. However, teachers whose classrooms are based on *power over* practices often don't perceive co-operation to be the two-way working relationship with students that the word implies. They see it as a one-way street in which students do what teachers want them to do. When students don't do what is expected, they are called "uncooperative," written up for bad behavior, sent to the principal's office to suffer consequences—or given rewards or incentives to do things the teacher's way.

The *co-* in *co*-operation means "together," and the *oper-* means "work," so *co-operation* means "working together." True co-operation is not something that can be mandated. Where there is no *togetherness* in the operation of a classroom—in mutual decision making, objective setting and problem solving—the following natural consequences can be expected: fear, resistance, arguments, hurt feelings, battles of will and other forms of conflict in addition to a reliance on punishment and rewards.

A fundamental law of human relations is this: Teachers who leave the *co-* out of classroom operations are destined to reap the consequences of the omission. No *co-* in classroom operations predicts a cycle in which conflict is followed by punishments and incentives to resolve the conflict, which leads to further conflict and further punishments and incentives, and on and on. If you aren't willing to work with your students, they aren't going to be willing to work with you.

Conversely, when you are willing to work with your students, you will find they enjoy working with you. According to leading scientists, co-operation is in our genes, since it is necessary for ongoing survival of a species. Humans have a feel-good response when co-operating with one another toward a shared objective or vision. And so, we do not have to teach young people co-operation—only inspire it by co-operating with them and giving them many opportunities to enjoy co-operative endeavors that have meaning and purpose for them. This is a definition we enjoy for *co-operation*: "A way to engage power with others so everyone has power to thrive."

What Is Your Vision for Your Classroom?

It is extremely helpful to have a Vision of your own to further strengthen the foundation you are establishing for your No-Fault Classroom. When you have a well-defined Vision, you are able to sense and articulate your purpose for teaching. With that clarity, you will be able to choose the methods and materials that will serve your Vision best.

Some things to consider: Do you want a classroom where students always get their work done your way and on your time schedule? Do you want a classroom where children follow rules—your rules? Think it through. If you say this is the kind of classroom you want, realize that you are likely choosing to spend a lot of your time looking for misbehavior, writing it up, reporting it to parents, sending students out of the room for it, collecting names of the unruly on the board, putting check marks next to them for each additional unacceptable behavior, and trying to determine appropriate rewards and punishments. Another major portion of your time will be spent trying to manage the students who complain, nag, bully, tattle and resist your efforts.

If your focus is on connecting with students, making relationships with them and finding out the good reasons they have for doing what they do, you are likely to spend very little of your time carrying out the above routines and a lot of your time in productive living and learning together.

Parker Palmer, author of *The Courage to Teach*, asked students from all around the country to describe a good teacher. He says that all of them described good teachers as people who have some sort of connective capacity, who connect themselves to their students, their students to one another, and everyone to the subject being studied. "The connections made by good teachers are held not in their methods but in their hearts . . . the place where intellect and emotion and spirit and will converge."[1]

Your Vision will be your pole star. Develop it carefully and align with it as many methods and practices as possible.

Here are two brief Classroom Vision statements written by teachers:

My Vision is a classroom where everyone's needs matter, where everyone enjoys learning and where we learn together to resolve conflicts peacefully.

My Vision is a learning environment where students feel physically and emotionally safe—a place where students know they belong, where their needs matter, their gifts, talents and ideas are received and celebrated, and they thrive as learners.

---

1. Palmer, *The Courage to Teach*, 11.

Be bold: set a Vision for the classroom you really want. What is the space like? The learning? What are the interactions like between you and your students? What are the interactions like between and among students?

My Vision is:

_____

_____

_____

_____

_____

_____

_____

_____

Lay The Foundation for Your No-Fault Classroom

When you have taken some time for reflection and are ready to lay the foundation for your No-Fault Classroom, we recommend you start with the two Class Meetings described below, before beginning the Introduction to the No-Fault Zone and the modules of the *No-Fault Classroom* curriculum.

Power is created not when some people coerce others but when they willingly take action together in support of a common purpose. Power corresponds to the human ability not just to act but to act in concert.

—Hannah Arendt

Class Meeting 1: Generate a Classroom Vision

When you take the time to form an understanding and agreement *with* your students about what kind of classroom you want to create, they receive the message, loud and clear, that their needs matter and that you value their thoughts. They will see and feel themselves to be active, integral contributors to their classroom rather than passive receivers of instructions, commands and demands. This is a powerful message that encourages students to take interest and participate in their learning community.

In Class Meeting 1, you will introduce to your students the value you see in creating a Vision and ask students for their ideas of how a Vision can serve them. Here are the values we see: a shared Vision clarifies what you want for yourself and for others, and it helps you direct your actions toward what you want. You will be creating your classroom together throughout the year, so sharing information about what you want and need is vital information at the beginning and throughout the year.

Generating a Classroom Vision can take a while, so please make time for it. Class Meeting 1 can also be planned to span a few sessions over the first week or two of school. We consider it an essential activity for constructing a No-Fault Classroom and hope you prioritize sufficient time for you and your class to meet.

Objective: To share your Vision and ask students to share their Visions for a classroom you would enjoy spending time in every day; to establish a community where everyone's Vision is included; to establish an intention for the classroom to be a place where everyone belongs; to focus minds on what you want to create during the school year; to listen to your students

Materials: Notes from Vision exercise, drawing paper, colored pencils and markers

We are disturbed not by what happens to us, but by our thoughts about what happens.

—Epictetus

Procedure:

1. Using your notes from the Vision exercise in Section I: Lay the Foundation for Your No-Fault Classroom, share your Vision with your students. Ask if they have questions about what you shared.

2. Lead students in a thought exercise to clarify their Vision for the classroom. You can ask them to close their eyes and picture what a welcoming learning community would look like: *What would you find in it? What could happen there? How would you feel when you walk in each morning?*

3. After finishing the visualization, hand out drawing paper to each student and ask them to record information about their Vision for the classroom. They can write their Vision down, make a list of attributes, draw a picture of it, write a poem, make a collage and so forth.

4. When finished, ask if any students will volunteer to show and share their Vision for the classroom.

5. Collect all Visions and make a collage, "quilt" or mandala with them, displaying them on the wall.

6. Take a photograph of the collage to place with your classroom Group Agreements (see Class Meeting 2) and for reference when the collage is taken down. (Please keep a copy of your original Classroom Vision collage pieces. You will refer to this Vision throughout the curriculum, including in some of the last few modules.)

Class Meeting 2: Facilitate Group Agreements

Often, in traditional classrooms, "group agreements" and rules are made arbitrarily and casually, if not unilaterally. Students say yes to rules they don't genuinely participate in making, nor think much about, then later receive punishment when they "break the rule."

In a relationship-based, No-Fault Classroom, Group Agreements are made to serve your Classroom Vision. When all members of the class come to a mutual understanding of what makes a safe learning environment, you have provided another experience that tells them that their needs matter and that they have a voice in how things run. Participating in making their own safety "rules" encourages students to express their needs, take responsibility for their behavior, take learning risks (make mistakes) and co-operate to create a community where everyone belongs and enjoys learning together.

Objective: To create an environment where students participate eagerly in learning tasks; to meet needs for physical and emotional safety and respect; to make agreements that everyone participates in and is willing to try; to acknowledge that all agreements are experiments in living and can be reviewed and revised if they are not working well; to reach genuine agreement that everyone assumes responsibility for them

Materials: Large chart paper prepared with large version of diagram below on it, copy of physical and emotional safety facts (below) for reference during discussion, markers, extra blank chart paper for lists of suggestions

Procedure:

1. Express to your students your desire to make your classroom safe for everyone. Share the science behind this recognition: that physical and emotional safety is essential for learning to take place. Share information from the scientific facts (below) in a way that your students will understand.

2. Post the chart paper with the diagram below reproduced on it somewhere where everyone can see it.

3. Lead a discussion about the need for physical safety. Ask students: *What actions are not physically safe in the classroom?* Write their answers, or ask a student to volunteer to write answers, on the chart on the left side and outside of the circle.

4. Turn the discussion to the need for emotional safety. Ask students: *What actions do not contribute to emotional safety?* Write their answers,

or ask a student to volunteer to write answers, on the chart on the right side and outside the circle.

5. By now some students will likely be wondering what the big empty circle on the chart is for. This is where you will make Group Agreements to meet needs for safety, trust and respect. Share your purpose for making Group Agreements together at the start of the year, and wanting to review them throughout the year. Here are some values we see in Group Agreements: establishing shared participation and responsibility; confirming clarity about the shared Vision for the classroom; establishing guidelines for safety, trust and respect that will allow optimal learning to take place.

6. Ask students to suggest actions they would like the group to consider for the Group Agreements. Help them get to specific doable requests, as much as possible. If someone says, *I want people to respect me*, you can ask: *What would you like people to agree to do that would meet your need for respect?* See also the list of sample Group Agreements below for examples of doable requests. It is difficult to "do" something abstract such as "always be respectful."

7. Make a list of suggestions on a blank piece of chart paper. Then go through each one and ask if anyone has questions about it. If not, ask if anyone is *not* willing to agree to that request. (This question is more likely to bring out any objections than if you ask, *Does everyone agree to this request?* With the positively-phrased question you are likely to get some unthinking compliance, since that is what many students are used to.) It is in the interest of the class to encourage questions and draw out any objections during this meeting or you will deal with them later on, most likely in the form of resistance or resentment.

8. Write all Group Agreements approved by the whole class in the circle in the center of the original chart.

9. Post your Group Agreements where everyone can see them. The Classroom Group Agreements are there to serve your Classroom Vision and meet people's needs for safety, trust, belonging, learning and more. Tell your students that the class will review them throughout the year. New agreements can be added, and old ones that don't work can be removed. Seeing the Group Agreements as life-enriching requests instead of set-in-stone demands makes it much more likely that you and your students will honor them. (Remember to keep a copy of your original Classroom Vision and Group Agreements on hand. You will refer to them throughout the curriculum, including in some of the last few modules.)

Facts about physical and emotional safety and learning

Physical and Emotional Safety is the number one requirement for learning to take place. Our brains are finely tuned to keep us safe at all times. There are three primary divisions of the brain—the primitive/old brain, the limbic brain and the reasoning/learning zones. When we sense danger, whether it is physical or emotional, real or imagined, fear is triggered. Fear has a dramatic effect on the body and the brain. To meet needs for protection and safety, stress hormones are automatically secreted throughout the body. In the face of perceived danger, quick action is more important than careful thinking and analysis. The reasoning and learning zones of the brain shut down. Energy goes to the survival zone of the brain at the base of the skull and to the arms and legs so we can protect ourselves by fighting or running away. In *Emotional Intelligence* by Daniel Goleman, this automatic process is referred to as an "emotional hijacking."

Understand the enemy and you can defeat him, understand yourself and there is no enemy.

—Ancient Chinese Proverb

Physical and emotional safety diagram for Class Meeting 2

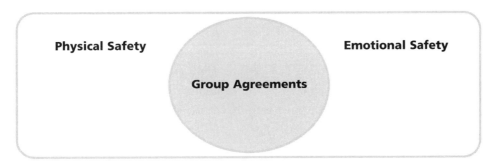

Sample Group Agreements

- ☐ Listen when others are talking.
- ☐ Use words to solve problems rather than kicking, hitting or harming others.
- ☐ Pick up after yourself.
- ☐ Don't laugh or tease when people make mistakes.
- ☐ No put-downs.
- ☐ Speak up when you'd like to see changes.

When Students Break an Agreement

The high price of punishment

In traditional settings where rules are made by teachers, when a student breaks a rule, the teacher typically gives a warning, makes a threat or determines a punishment which is meant to instill fear and obedience. The result of these strategies for compliance is a class full of students who feel guilty and ashamed or resentful and angry. With these feelings stirring, it becomes unlikely that students will wholeheartedly attend to learning of any kind. The feelings inspired by such policies and practices show up in the classroom as resistance, or half-hearted compliance.

Another result of seeing punitive practices such as warnings, threats and punishments modeled by adults is that students learn to use the same strategies with each other, in the classroom and on the playground. Students who use threats and punishment to get other kids to do what they want are called "bullies." Anti-bullying programs now abound to change this behavior; they often administer bigger doses of guilt, shame and punishment in hopes that the delinquent students will change their ways. Surprisingly few people ask the question, *Where do these students learn bullying behavior?* Fewer still see any correlation between disciplinary policies and bullying. And, tragically, disciplinary policies rarely get to the root of the problem. These policies neither help students identify the needs they want to meet nor do they help them find truly effective ways to meet them.

An alternative to punishment

When students participate in making Group Agreements for the classroom, in order to meet their needs for safety, trust, respect and learning, they tend to take responsibility from the start for the Agreements and for their own behavior. Group Agreements assure students that their needs are taken seriously, their word is trusted, and their thoughts and concerns are valued. When every student has agreed to the proposed Agreements, you can move forward with assurance that if agreements are broken there will be a good reason that can be discussed, rather than thinking that students who break Agreements are disrespectful, rebellious or "bad."

> **If you want to teach people a new way of thinking, don't bother trying to teach them. Instead, give them a tool, the use of which will lead to new ways of thinking.**
>
> —Buckminster Fuller

Identify Needs & Strategies for Meeting Them

Here is a routine we suggest for times when students break classroom Agreements.

1. Student breaks an agreement.

2. If someone is in danger, use protective force or restraint, if necessary.

3. Provide time if necessary for an Energy Shifter (see Appendix 3) so the student can cool down before talking more.

4. Give empathy for the student's feelings and needs.

5. When the student knows what his or her needs are in the situation, they will be able to see other, more effective, ways to handle those needs. They will also be able to imagine what they could do differently in the future for better results.

Example 1

Teacher: Rylan, I see how difficult it is for you to follow through on your agreement to listen while others are talking, and some of the other students and I would like to hear what is preventing you from doing what you agreed.

Rylan: I just get so frustrated sitting and listening all the time. I need to be able to do something, so I just start talking to Lisa.

Teacher: So, you are saying that you feel pent up and frustrated when you are listening for long periods of time, is that right?

Rylan: Yeah!

Teacher: And you need something to do?

Rylan: Yeah!

Teacher: I have an idea. Do you think it would help you to listen while others are talking if you were able to quietly doodle on paper or squeeze a ball?

Rylan: Maybe.

Teacher: Would you be willing to try that for a few days and let me know how that works?

Rylan: Okay.

Example 2

[Teacher restrains Angela from hitting Jon.]

Teacher: Angela, I can't let you hit Jon. I am stopping you because we agreed to make this a safe place for everyone, and I will stop anyone who tries to hit another student. It looks like you are really upset, and I wonder what you need right now.

Angela: I need him to stop calling me names.

Teacher: Are you feeling upset because you need consideration and respect?

Angela: Yeah! And he's not following the rule we made not to call people names.

Teacher: Hmm? Are you saying that you need to be able to trust people to follow through on what they say they will do?

Angela: Yeah! If Jon doesn't have to follow the rules, I don't have to either.

Teacher: Are you saying that if there are rules you want everyone to follow them?

Angela: Yes!

Teacher: Would you be willing to talk with Jon about this?

Angela: No. He won't listen to me.

Teacher: If I stay with you for support?

Angela: I'll try it, but I'm not so sure it will work.

Teacher: I appreciate your willingness to try. Shall we find Jon and make an appointment to talk with him?

You may think that this approach will take time away from learning. However, it takes much less time than punitive practices do, and students will see you modeling problem-solving strategies that they will gradually learn and use themselves.

> Although attempting to bring about world peace through the internal transformation of individuals is difficult, it is the only way.
>
> —His Holiness the Dalai Lama

Supporting Activities

- Provide two shoe boxes for the classroom. Label one "**What's Working**," and the other, "**What Isn't Working**." Students can decorate them if they like. Encourage students to express themselves by writing their appreciations and complaints about what is going on in the classroom and putting them in the appropriate boxes. Agree upon a time and format for reading them. Celebrate appreciations and problem-solve complaints.

- Provide a stack of Notes of Appreciation (template in Appendix 2). Use them to write notes to students about how their actions contribute to your life and/or to life in the classroom. Encourage students to write notes to each other to express how individual and group actions affect them.

SECTION II

Construction Materials

Setting up Your No-Fault Construction Zone

Scripts, Facts & Messages

The Twins introduce every Power and every module with a Narrative: Notes from the No-Fault Zone. They also deliver Facts, which are the key points of the modules, and a Message, which gives suggestions about what to do to develop the Power.

Students volunteer to read the roles of the Twins in the Notes from the No-Fault Zone, Facts and Message that are in every module. As many as four students can read during each module: one to read the script for Nao, one for Michi, one to read the Facts, and one to read the Message. Alternatively, two students could do all the reading: the student reading Nao's part would read the Facts and the student reading Michi's part would read the Message. Some students might enjoy wearing a hat, a cape or costume item of their choosing to help them take on the role they will play.

You will find Notes from the No-Fault Zone scripts at the beginning of each module. Facts and Messages are found at the beginning of each module immediately following the Narrative.

Tip: Scripts will need to be photocopied for each reader.

Tip: The Facts and Message for each module will need to be photocopied for students to read and to be posted in the classroom.

No-Fault Construction Zone

It will be helpful to provide a special place in the classroom to be the center of the curriculum activities, if only a table or counter with a little wall space above it. You will need a message station, a construction area and a reference area. Put open-top boxes, like shoe boxes, for "What's Working" and "What Isn't Working," and the Notes of Appreciation in this same general area. Give the space its own special name: Communication Central (CC) or Conflict Prevention & Resolution Central (CPRC) or No-Fault Construction Zone, or whatever you and your students choose. (We will refer to this space as the No-Fault Construction Zone from now on.)

Message Station

We suggest that you post the Facts and Message from the Twins on a bulletin board in the morning, before beginning a *No-Fault Classroom* module, as if a correspondence has just arrived from the Twins. If possible, the bulletin board or message station could be stationed above the cards, pencils, markers and so forth that students use to construct their materials.

Construction Area

It is important to have construction supplies available during the entire time that your class is engaged in the *No-Fault Classroom* curriculum. Card Decks will be added to regularly, cards will be lost or misplaced and need replacement, and some students may want to add to or reconstruct a rumpled IOS Power Panel.

Reference Area

There are a number of posters and charts that will be made by you and/or your students to remind students of new concepts and provide easy reference. Some students might want to decorate or illustrate the posters to enhance the themes. It would be wonderful to paper the walls with them. However, if wall space is limited, make the posters on flip-chart paper that has adhesive at the top. Choose one place on a wall for posters and place one atop the other—with the most relevant information for the week at the top. When you or your students want to refer to a different poster, bring it to the top or page through the stack to find the information needed.

Materials

Options for Materials Construction

The *No-Fault Classroom* curriculum requires a set of materials that students and teacher will use throughout the school year. It is important that teachers look over the list of materials in this section and decide how they want to gather and produce them for their classroom.

There are three ways to produce the materials you will need for this curriculum:

1. Copy and cut out the templates in this section. (The IOS Power Panel will need to be enlarged to the size of students' desk spaces.)

2. Use the templates in this section as models for students to design and make their own materials.

3. Purchase professionally produced materials from Kindle-Hart Communication.

If you choose to have students make their own materials, you may want to divide the class into small construction teams—making sure that there are construction enthusiasts in each team. Keep it light, keep it fun, keep it moving. Lists of materials and supplies can be found in the Teacher Preparation pages at the beginning of each Power. Directions for constructing materials are integrated into each module's activities. Most of the construction takes place in the first eight modules.

Supplies for Materials Construction

for General Use

- ❑ Three boxes with open tops for notes
- ❑ Bulletin board or wall space to post Facts and Messages
- ❑ Colored pencils, crayons and markers
- ❑ Drawing paper
- ❑ Push pins, blue tape
- ❑ Scissors

for IOS Power Panels

- ❑ 18" x 22" piece of white construction paper for each student
- ❑ Markers in black and 5 different colors
- ❑ Small objects, such as small rocks or game tokens (students can each bring their own from home)

Tip: Keep all posters and charts made during the *No-Fault Classroom* curriculum for use in future modules or for later reference.

for Card Decks

- ☐ 3" x 5" index cards in 4 different colors, 15–20 of each color per student

- ☐ (Yellow = Need Cards; pink = Feeling Cards; light blue = observations; white = Choice Cards)

for Charts

- ☐ Chart paper, flip chart, butcher paper or poster boards

- ☐ Bulletin board, easel or blue tape (to post charts)

- ☐ Markers

for Materials Storage

- ☐ 9" x 12" two-pocket folder or 10" x 14" manila envelope for each student's Power Panel & Cards

- ☐ Rubber bands for Card Decks, 4 per student

Templates for Materials Construction

The templates listed below are found in Appendix 2. In parentheses, you'll see the module in which the template, chart or worksheet is first used; many will be used for subsequent modules as well, and the Power Panel and Card Decks in particular will be used consistently throughout the modules.

Internal Operating System (IOS) Power Panel Template (Introduction to the No-Fault Zone)

Charts

- ☐ The 9 Powers (Introduction to the No-Fault Zone)

- ☐ 4 Ways to Listen (Module 6a)

- ☐ 6 Steps to D.E.F.U.S.E. Anger (Module 7b)

- ☐ 9 Steps to Solutions (Module 8a)

Card Decks

- ☐ 14 Choice Cards (Module 1b)
- ☐ 14 Need Cards (Module 2a)
- ☐ 14 Feeling Cards (Module 4a)

Worksheets

- ☐ Note of Appreciation (Class Meeting 2)
- ☐ Real-Life Experiment Log (Module 3b)
- ☐ The Feelings & Needs Connection (Module 4a)
- ☐ Feelings vs Thoughts (Module 4b)
- ☐ Observation & Thought Statement Flash Cards (Module 5a)

SECTION III

Construct Your No-Fault Classroom

Introduction to the No-Fault Zone

(60 minutes)

Objective: To introduce the curriculum; the No-Fault Zone; the Twins, Nao and Michi; the Internal Operating System Power Panel; and the 9 Powers

Materials: One sheet of 18" x 22" white or off-white construction paper for each student; colored pens, pencils or crayons; legal-size manila envelopes (2 per student, to store their folded IOS Power Panel & other materials); 1 colored IOS Power Panel to show students and/or several Power Panel templates for students to use as construction models; the 9 Powers Chart

Type of Activity: Construction

Vocabulary: These words are used in the Introduction to the No-Fault Zone and in upcoming modules. You may want to review these terms with your students before or during the session.

- No-Fault Zone
- 9 Powers
- exploration
- transmit, transmissions
- Internal Operating System (IOS)
- coordinates
- IOS Power Panel

- thermometer
- temperature
- crescent
- needs
- feelings
- observations
- Calm Alert

Procedure:

1. Get the materials listed above ready for construction.

2. Tell students the object of the lesson is to construct their Internal Operating System Power Panels.

3. Read the Letter from the Twins (below) to the class. In the letter, the Twins introduce themselves and explain their purpose. They also give an overview of the weeks ahead.

4. Guide students in constructing their own IOS Power Panel, as directed by the Twins.

Letter from the Twins

Hi! We're Michi, (pronounced Mee-chee) and Nao (pronounced Now). Well, I'm Nao, and Michi is my twin brother. We're sixteen years old, and we come from a little-known dimension called the No-Fault Zone.

We appreciate your giving us your precious time and attention today so we can introduce ourselves and tell you why we want to talk with you.

We have a lot we want to tell you about where we come from and also about the 9 Powers that Earthlings have. You can activate your 9 Powers and make life on Earth more wonderful in many, many ways.

If you could read our minds it would take no time at all to transmit what we have to share. However, since you can't read our minds, we are going to send you weekly written transmissions that will include Facts, Messages and Explorations that will take you on journeys into Inner Space.

Because we are Inner Space Explorers! Like astronauts are for Outer Space.

You all know something about Outer Space exploration, don't you? So you probably know that Earth is a living planet within a solar system, within a galaxy, in an expanding universe. There are thousands of satellites throughout Outer Space with high-tech instruments that collect information about the solar system and beyond. Earthling astronauts have, as you probably know, traveled into Outer Space, and some have even walked on the moon. They were the first Earthlings who took pictures of the planet Earth from Outer Space. As much information about Outer Space as you have in your libraries and computers right now, there is still mystery, and so much more to explore and learn about it.

We're here to tell you that there is just as much to explore and learn about Inner Space.

So where should we begin?

Our home, the No-Fault Zone, is a friendly place. In the No-Fault Zone, people really do care about each other and really do show it in many ways. All Earthlings can find their way to the No-Fault Zone, once they become aware of it and choose to go there. But it's invisible to the eye, which is probably why so many Earthlings don't know about it. During the weeks that we will be traveling Inner Space together, you will gradually learn more and more about the No-Fault Zone.

Earthlings are so busy, moving so fast and doing so many things that they usually don't have time to learn about the No-Fault Zone and to investigate it. Instead, Earthlings have developed habits that often make life less than wonderful. In fact too many Earthlings keep making themselves miserable with their arguments, conflicts and wars. All of this fighting has created a pretty big Fault Zone on Planet Earth. In the Fault Zone, black and white thinking rules, fingers point, words hurt, enemies are created, and fights and wars are expected at all times.

Michi and I feel sad to see this. Blame, threats, fighting and conflict make living and learning together hard to do. We're talking to you now because we'd like to see you Earthlings have more fun, get along better and have more time for learning new things. We'd like to see all Earthlings living satisfying, meaningful lives. After all, we're all in this Universe together, and the more Earthlings thrive and get along together, the more satisfying, fun and meaningful life will be for everyone.

We're all in this Universe together.

So we had the idea to correspond with students and teachers to try to explain the No-Fault Zone and the many Powers that Earthlings have. You aren't quite as busy as adult Earthlings: you have more time in a day to think, wonder and learn.

Your Internal Operating System (IOS)

One of the most important things we want to share with you is that all Earthlings have an Internal Operating System (or IOS) made up of Earthling needs, feelings, thoughts, observations and choices.

When you know how to read your IOS, you have the information you need to make wise choices about your life. In the No-Fault Zone, we receive messages about our IOS every moment. Actually, you do too, though you may not realize it, because most Earthlings have not yet learned about their IOS. And hardly any have learned how to access it.

There is an instrument on Earth called a Global Positioning System that is used in cars. It shows the coordinates of where an object is on Earth. It can locate you or anything else that you want to find.

There is also a finely tuned instrument that locates where you are in Inner Space. It is called the IOS Power Panel. It gives a read-out, each moment, of the state of your feelings, your thoughts, your needs and your ability to see the truth of things. You'll learn more about the importance of these read-outs when you see the IOS Power Panel and learn how to read it. We sent your teacher one to show you, and you can make your own.*

Today you will make your own IOS Power Panel so you can use it in the weeks ahead.

You can start anywhere you want to make your Power Panel. Follow the template your teacher is providing. We would like to recommend a few things:

First write the name of each of the areas on the Power Panel: needs, feelings and all the others.

After you have done this, we'd like you to color them.

While you are working, we will tell you about the different areas of the IOS Power Panel, and the colors that go with each area. There are also a few areas where you can choose your own color scheme.

◉   ◉   ◉

In this half circle in the middle you will be reading your needs. Please color that area yellow.

◉   ◉   ◉

The next crescent out from the Needs area is Feelings. Color the Feelings area red.

◉   ◉   ◉

Next to Feelings is Observations. Color this area blue.

◉   ◉   ◉

The big square that touches Observations is a space of Choices and Calm Alert. Color this space green.

◉   ◉   ◉

*Note: To construct the IOS Power Panels show students a colored IOS Power Panel or provide photocopies of the template in Appendix 2 for small groups of students to use as a blueprint. Guide students through the following process for constructing—drawing and coloring—their own Power Panels, as you continue to read the Twins' Notes below.

The strip along the bottom is called the Feeling Thermometer. This is where we will be reading the temperature of feelings. On the far left of the Thermometer is VERY COLD and on the far right of the Thermometer is VERY HOT. Color the thermometer in colors that represent hot and cold for you.

◉   ◉   ◉

The two areas of the Fault Zone on left and right is for a black-and-white world. Color it in black and white. You can use stripes, dots, a checkerboard or any other design you like.

Introduction to the 9 Powers

Imagine how helpful it could be to know what you need at each moment, and to know why you do what you do. Imagine what it would be like if you had the power to make each moment more interesting and fun for everyone. Imagine what it would be like if you had the power to turn arguments into helpful conversations, and if you knew how to peacefully resolve the conflicts that come up in your life. The truth is that you already have the 9 Powers that help you do amazing things like this, and more. But your Powers probably haven't been activated yet. With the help of your IOS, we're here to introduce you to your Powers and activate them.

Each week you will be exploring the 9 Powers that you have inside of you. Your IOS will give you read-outs on most of these Powers. As you explore and learn about the Powers, you will be able to activate them to make wise choices, prevent and resolve conflicts and generally make life more wonderful for you and for those around you.

These are your 9 Powers:

1. The Power to Get to Calm Alert

2. The Power to Know Your Needs

3. The Power to Meet Needs

4. The Power to Read Feelings

5. The Power to Observe

6. The Power to Listen

7. The Power to Navigate the Fault Zone

8. The Power to Co-operate to Solve Problems & Conflicts

9. The Power to Create a No-Fault Zone Wherever You Are

You might be thinking to yourself that these aren't really Powers. Maybe they don't sound special or like real magic. But we're here to tell you that these are the real powers that Earthlings possess. They're not Transformer powers or Martian powers or powers of beings from any other planet or galaxy. They are real powers that are yours to use for your entire life, if you are willing to activate them.

It takes a little time to get beyond what can be seen with your eyes, but that's where Earthling Powers lie. Maybe it sounds a bit confusing and mysterious right now, but remember that much more will be revealed about your Powers during the weeks we travel together.

It takes a little time to get below the surface of things but that's where Earthling Powers lie.

Supporting Activities:

- Give students time during the week to complete work on their Power Panels.

- Give each student a 10" x 14" manila envelope in which to keep their Power Panels and other materials they will be constructing and using in future modules.

- Ask for volunteers to make 2 to 4 IOS Power Panels for classroom use. The classroom Power Panels can be laminated for durability and used in a variety of ways during the year. It may also be useful to have a Power Panel that is large enough to post on the wall for reference during activities.

POWER 1 · **The Power to Get to Calm Alert**

TEACHER PREPARATION

Advance Preparation for Modules 1a and 1b

☐ Assemble the materials required for each module (see Materials lists on the pages that follow).

☐ Photocopy the Notes from the No-Fault Zone narrative script from both modules for two to four student readers.

☐ Photocopy the Facts and Message for both modules.

☐ Post the Facts and Message for Module 1a at your classroom Message Station at the beginning of the day you will cover Module 1a.

☐ Post the Facts and Message for Module 1b at your classroom Message Station at the beginning of the day you will cover Module 1b.

Earthlings function best when in a state of Calm Alert.

Vocabulary for Power 1

(These words are used in Modules 1a and 1b and in following modules. You may want to review these terms with your students before or during the modules.)

- Calm Alert
- Feeling Thermometer
- read-out
- function (as in physical or mechanical functions, not mathematical functions)
- well-being
- optimal, optimum functioning
- experiment
- digestion
- circulation (as the biological system)
- respiration
- elimination (as the biological system)
- Body Scan
- shift energy
- Energy Shifters
- choice
- frontal lobes (of the brain)

Module 1a: Your Feeling Thermometer

Objective: To increase self-awareness and well-being by learning to read feelings on a Feeling Thermometer and learning ways to get to Calm Alert

Activities:

☐ Volunteers read Notes from the No-Fault Zone, Facts and Message (15 minutes)

☐ Exploration: *Feeling Thermometer Check* (25 minutes)

Type of Activity: Teacher-led exercise

☐ Exploration: *Hot or Cold?* (20 minutes)

Type of Activity: Teacher-led discussion

☐ Follow-on Exploration: *Body Scan* (10-minute optional exercise for a different day than the day you do Module 1a)

Type of Activity: Guided visualization

Materials:

✔ Materials to prepare in advance: None

✔ Materials for construction: None

Materials to be constructed in class during Module 1a:

☐ Tokens (each student will choose a small object to use with their Feeling Thermometer)

Materials constructed previously to be used in Module 1a:

☐ IOS Power Panels for each student

✔ Materials to be used in the Follow-on Exploration: None

You can get a moment-to-moment read-out about the intensity of your feelings.

Module 1b: Energy Shifting

Objective: To increase choice and effectiveness by noticing feeling states (hot feelings versus cold feelings versus Calm Alert) and by learning to shift energy for optimum functioning (to get to a state of Calm Alert)

Activities:

- [ ] Volunteers read Notes from the No-Fault Zone, Facts and Message (10 minutes)

- [ ] Materials Construction: Choice Cards (5 minutes)

- [ ] Exploration: *Energy Shifting* (10 minutes)

  Type of Activity: Teacher-led discussion

- [ ] Exploration: *Heart Lock-In Energy Shifter* (10 minutes)

  Type of Activity: Guided Energy-Shifting (relaxation) exercise, appreciation

- [ ] Exploration: *Energy-Shifting Exercises Chart* (25 minutes)

  Type of Activity: Class discussion, small-group charting

Materials:

Materials to prepare in advance:

- [ ] Photocopies (1 set) of the one-page directions for the Energy-Shifting exercises in Appendix 3

Materials for construction:

- [ ] Chart paper

- [ ] Easel or blue tape (or use a flip chart)

- [ ] White 3" x 5" index cards (1 per student)

- [ ] Pens or markers

Materials to be constructed in class during Module 1b:

- [ ] Energy-Shifting Exercises Chart

- [ ] Choice Cards (using the white index cards and pens or markers)

Materials constructed previously to be used in Module 1b:

- [ ] IOS Power Panels, Feeling Thermometer tokens

> Choices are a big part of your IOS.

Module 1a: Your Feeling Thermometer

Notes from the No-Fault Zone

Nao: Hi! Michi and I are excited to explore the Powers with you, starting with the first one: the Power to Get to Calm Alert.

Michi: The first place in your Internal Operating System we want you to get familiar with is Calm Alert. Please find Calm Alert on your IOS Power Panel.

Nao: You notice it's in the middle of your Feeling Thermometer. That's because it is a center point, a place where you feel calm and alert at the same time. Do you know this feeling? We'll get to experience it soon.

Michi: Some people experience Calm Alert as a sense of focus, balance, being very present. It's a feeling-and-mind state that lets you think clearly or be "on" or "in the zone" when you're playing sports or playing an instrument. The Power to Get to Calm Alert can help you do your best in any situation.

Nao: Your Feeling Thermometer is a fine-tuned instrument that tells you how far you are from Calm Alert. You'll be able to get a read-out whenever you want, once you learn how it works.

Michi: On the Feeling Thermometer, you read the temperature of your feelings and notice when they are so hot or so cold that you are not able to function well.

Nao: Because most Earthlings aren't aware of their Feeling Thermometer, they often don't notice feelings until they get way hot or way cold. By then they are usually upset, angry or shut down. Then they can't think clearly enough to make wise choices.

Michi: We hope you will check out your Feeling Thermometer and see for yourself what it can do for you.

POWER 1a

FACTS

⊙ Earthlings function best when in a state of Calm Alert.

⊙ Knowing how to get to Calm Alert is an important skill for Earthlings.

⊙ Earthlings have access to many choices for action when in a state of Calm Alert.

⊙ Certain kinds of thoughts take Earthlings out of a state of Calm Alert into a Fault Zone filled with stress pools, anger volcanoes and black holes of conflict.

POWER 1a

MESSAGE

- Use your IOS Feeling Thermometer to get a moment-to-moment read-out about the intensity of your feelings.

- Learn to read your Feeling Thermometer to find out how far you are from Calm Alert.

- Learn ways to get to Calm Alert whenever you choose to.

Exploration: *Feeling Thermometer Check* (25 minutes)

Objective: To learn to read a Feeling Thermometer and receive important information about well-being

Materials: IOS Power Panels, student tokens (such as a small stone, paper clip, penny), list of statements (provided below)

Type of Activity: Teacher-led exercise

Procedure:

1. Ask students to get out their Internal Operating System (IOS) Power Panels and place them in front of them.

2. Ask students to each select a token (a small object such as a paper clip, penny, small rock or shell) to use as a marker on their Power Panel.

3. Review the Feeling Thermometer function. Ask students: *What did the Twins say about the Feeling Thermometer? How can the Feeling Thermometer be useful to us?*

4. Experiment with the Feeling Thermometer: Read the statements below out loud, one at a time, or ask for a student volunteer to read them.

5. After each statement is read, ask students to place their token in the area of the Feeling Thermometer on their IOS Power Panel that they guess best matches the temperature of the statement.

6. After students have a moment to place their token for the current statement, ask them to share their guesses. Then, read the next statement and repeat.

Statements for *Feeling Thermometer Check*

"I'm furious."

"I don't know what I'm feeling."

"I don't have any feelings."

"I want to scream."

"I can see what to do."

"I'm scared and don't know what to do."

"I feel confident."

Exploration: *Hot or Cold?* (20 minutes)

Objective: To identify different energy states

Materials: Scenarios (provided below), IOS Power Panels, tokens for Feeling Thermometer

Type of Activity: Teacher-led discussion

Procedure:

1. Read a hypothetical scenario from those provided below, or choose instead a scenario from your literature or history lessons.

2. Ask students to imagine the temperature and intensity of the character's feelings and put a token on that spot on their Feeling Thermometer.

3. Ask students if any will volunteer to share what they came up with. If students have different answers, tell them this is natural. Reinforce the fact that we don't know for sure how other people are feeling; we can only guess.

Scenarios for *Hot or Cold?*

A mother sees her son sitting on the sofa with shoulders slumped. He is staring at the floor. He has been sitting there for an hour. She asks, *Are you feeling sad?* He answers, slowly, *I don't know.*

Shona enters her house, red in the face and panting as if she has run all the way home. She slams the door after her and races up the stairs shouting, *Leave me alone.*

Simon wakes up suddenly in the middle of the night from a dream where he was being chased by a pack of wolves. He is breathing hard. He tries to get out of bed but can't seem to move his body.

Arun sits at his desk and pretends to listen to another student give a report. Arun hasn't heard one word of the report because he is caught up in thinking about something that happened earlier in the day. Thoughts like: *He shouldn't have done that! It's not fair. He's a jerk!!* are fast and furious and create a thought storm for Arun.

Maxine is excited to go to the lake with her family for the weekend, to swim and fish. But when she gets home from school on Friday, her mother is sick and says they'll have to go another time. Without saying a word, Maxine turns on the TV and sits staring at it for the next two hours.

Supporting Activities

- Teacher Practice: Check your own Feeling Thermometer several times a day. When you do, STOP (or slow down) and take a read-out of your feeling temperature in the current moment. What do you notice?

- During each day this week, ask students to stop and notice the temperature of their feelings and put a finger or a marker on their Feeling Thermometer. What do you notice?

Follow-on Exploration: *Body Scan* (10 minutes)

Objective: To learn to notice the sensations/signals in your body

Materials: IOS Power Panels, tokens for the Feeling Thermometer

Type of Activity: Guided visualization

Procedure:

1. Read this review to the class or review in your own words: *Our bodies are busy every moment regulating our physical systems (such as digestion, circulation, respiration and elimination) to maintain our balance and well-being.*

   We get signals from these systems letting us know when they are challenged—we get a stomachache when digestion is not smooth, and numb hands or feet when circulation is not working optimally.

   As we have discussed, we also get signals from our Internal Operating System about how things are going in our Inner Space: we get feelings of happiness and satisfaction as well as feelings of stress, anger and sadness.

   When we notice our feelings and learn to use our Feeling Thermometer we have more choice about how we feel and what we do.

2. Read this introduction to the class or use your own words: *Today I'd like to conduct an experiment together. The purpose of the experiment is to increase our ability to notice feelings and feeling temperatures. I will be asking you to sit straight in a comfortable way, close your eyes and allow me to guide you into an Inner Space exploration called a Body Scan. After*

we're done, we'll have a short time to talk about the experiment if you would like. So, if you're willing to try this experiment with me, here's what we'll do:

3. Read the guided visualization below to your students.

> Sit on your chair with both feet on the floor with your hands on your knees. Close your eyes. Take a few deep breaths.

> Bring your attention to your head and neck. Move your head up and down, side to side, and in circles. Feel the heaviness of it. Let it hang forward and relax.

> Put your attention on your shoulders. Lift them up and down, move them front and back and in circles. Wiggle them. Relax them.

> Lift your arms. Wiggle them and shake them out. Rest them at your side or with your hands on your knees.

> Shake your hands out, and wiggle your fingers and relax them.

> Stretch your legs in front of you. Tighten them and relax them two or three times. Shake them.

> Make circles with your feet, one direction then the other. Place your feet on the floor.

> Wiggle your toes. Point them and relax them. Place your feet on the floor again.

> Stop to listen to your body. What word comes up to describe the general feeling of your body? Light? Heavy? Notice your head and neck, shoulders, arms, fingers and hands, legs and ankles, feet and toes.

> Take five or six deep breaths and then open your eyes.

4. Check in with students, ask if any want to discuss the results of the experiment: *What did you notice?*

5. If it seems useful, try this experiment another day with students standing up, and also, if there's room, try it sometime with all students lying down on the floor.

Module 1b: Energy Shifting

Notes from the No-Fault Zone

Nao: We hope you've been using your Feeling Thermometer during the week so you can get moment-to-moment read-outs and notice when your feelings are very hot or very cold.

Michi: It's helpful to know this because when your feelings are Very Cold, you might freeze up or numb out, feel like you're in a fog, or not feel anything at all. This makes it hard to take action.

Nao: And when your feelings are Very Hot, you might experience heat in your head or your chest, you might feel a rush of energy in your body that makes you want to punch, hit, yell or run. Then it's hard to think clearly or do what's best for you.

Michi: Since Calm Alert is the temperature setting in the IOS where everyone functions best, people all over the world have exercises to shift energy from Hot to Calm Alert or from Cold to Calm Alert. We call these exercises Energy Shifters. You probably know some of these, and we've got some more for you to try. See how many Energy Shifters you can find that work for you to shift your energy.

Nao: When you learn how to shift energy, that's a choice you will have for the rest of your life. Choices are a big part of your IOS. Today we're sending you your first of fourteen Choice Cards. Your first Choice Card will say: "**Energy Shift: Get to Calm Alert.**"

Materials Construction: *Choice Cards* (5 minutes)

1. If you have purchased or made Choice Cards in advance, hand each student an "**Energy Shift: Get to Calm Alert**" Choice Card. If not, students will make their first Choice Card now.

2. If students are making their own cards, hand each student one white 3" x 5" index card.

3. Ask students to fold their card in half lengthwise so that they can cut on the fold to make two 3" x 2.5" cards. Write on the board, "**Energy Shift: Get to Calm Alert**," and ask students to write it on one of their two cards. Ask them to save the other card in their envelope for a later module.*

4. When everyone has their Choice Card, go on to read the Facts for Module 1b.

*Note: All subsequent Choice, Feeling and Need cards will be made this way.

POWER 1b

FACTS

⊙ When Earthlings think thoughts that stimulate stress, anger or fear, up to 80 percent of their usual blood supply can leave the thinking center of the brain (the frontal lobes). Then thinking becomes fuzzy, feelings get intense and Earthlings cannot function well.

⊙ Fortunately, throughout history and in all cultures Earthlings have devised Energy-Shifting exercises to help them get to Calm Alert and optimum functioning.

POWER 1b

MESSAGE

When you want to get to Calm Alert:

- Take a read of your Feeling Thermometer.

- Notice when your feelings are very hot or very cold.

- Do Energy-Shifting exercises.

Exploration: *Energy Shifting* (10 minutes)

Objective: To explore and clarify the purpose of Energy Shifting

Materials: None

Type of Activity: Teacher-led discussion

Procedure:

1. Read this review to the class or review in your own words: *When you see that your feelings are outside of Calm Alert, your power zone, you can use Energy-Shifting exercises to get back to Calm Alert.*

2. Ask students to share their ideas about the following questions:
   Why would you want to shift energy?
   What makes it difficult to shift energy when feelings are very hot?
   What makes it difficult to shift energy when feelings are very cold?
   What could help you remember your Power to shift energy to Get to Calm Alert?

Exploration: *Heart Breathing Energy Shifter*[1] (10 minutes)

Objective: To learn a way to shift energy to get to Calm Alert

Materials: None

Type of Activity: Guided Energy-Shifting (relaxation) exercise, appreciation

Procedure:

1. Ask students to think of something they are grateful for, something that makes them smile. It could be a pet, a person, a tree or flower.

2. Read students the following short visualization:
   - Sit comfortably, close your eyes and relax.
   - Take five slow breaths.
   - Place your hands on the center of your chest.
   - Think of the person, pet or plant that makes you smile. Breathe in the smiling, grateful energy. Breathe this feeling into the area under your hands.
   - Take five more slow breaths.

3. Use this exercise as a fallback when an energy shift is needed and/or as a way to start the morning with your students.

1. *This is a variation of a HeartMath exercise (www.heartmath.org). The HeartMath system was created by Doc Childre, a stress researcher, author and consultant to leaders in business, science and medicine. HeartMath offers an innovative view of psychology, physiology and human potential that provides a new model for efficient living in the modern world. HeartMath is taught in schools, corporations, government agencies and health care institutions to give people the ability to meet life challenges with resiliency, intelligence and compassion.*

Exploration: *Energy-Shifting Exercises Chart* (25 minutes)

Objective: To experiment with different ways to shift energy; To find energy-shifting strategies that help students get to Calm Alert

Materials: Chart paper, easel or blue tape (or use a flip chart), markers, a set of copies of the one-page directions for Energy Shifters from Appendix 3

Type of Activity: Class discussion, small-group charting

Procedure:

1. Get out a piece of chart paper or an empty page on a flip chart for a class chart of Energy-Shifting exercises.

2. Brainstorm ways to shift energy with the whole class.

   These are suggestions you might expect students to come up with:

   Take a Body Scan, stop and stretch, stop and breathe, take a walk or run, find someone you trust to talk with, listen to music, sing, play an instrument, draw, paint, play with clay, put music on and dance

3. Record ideas on the chart and keep it up in the room.

4. Add the Energy-Shifting exercises from Step 6 below to the chart.

5. Continue to add to the chart throughout the year.

6. Add the following Energy Shifters to the chart:

   Heart Breathing, The Hook-Up, Tekubi Furi (hand shaking), Cross Crawl, The Neurovascular Hold, The Tree, 6-Second Pause, Self-Empathy

7. Divide the class into four or five small groups

8. Give each group the directions (from Appendix 3) for one of the eight Energy-Shifting exercises you wrote on the chart (below). Explain that each group will learn their exercise and prepare to teach it to the class.

9. Set up a schedule so each group has a time to teach the class their exercise within the next 2–3 weeks.

The exercises on this list come from a variety of sources and have helped people on all continents and through the ages tap into their power to shift their energy, change the temperature of their feelings and get to Calm Alert. Professional athletes learn and use these kinds of exercises during training and competition.

We imagine you and your students will know or discover additional ways to get to Calm Alert that you can experiment with and share with classmates.

Energy-Shifting Exercises

Heart Breathing

The Hook-Up

Tekubi Furi (hand shaking)

Cross Crawl

The Neurovascular Hold

The Tree

6-Second Pause

Self-Empathy

Supporting Activities

- Teacher Practice: Try each of the Energy-Shifting exercises for yourself to add to your tools for getting to Calm Alert whenever you want to.

- After an Energy-Shifting exercise has been introduced, ask students during the following week if they have had opportunity to use it or if they have used any of the other Energy-Shifting exercises that have been introduced in class (or that they find on their own). Add new exercises to your class Energy-Shifting Exercises Chart.

- Make copies of the Energy-Shifting Exercise Log (see Appendix 3) for students to fill out if they want to record their experiments and discover which exercises work best for them.

POWER 2 ▪ **The Power to Know What You Need**

TEACHER PREPARATION

Advance Preparation for Modules 2a and 2b

☐ Assemble the materials required for each module (see Materials lists on the pages that follow).

☐ Photocopy the Notes from the No-Fault Zone narrative script from both modules for two to four student readers.

☐ Photocopy the Facts and Message for both modules.

☐ Post the Facts and Message for Module 2a at your classroom Message Station at the beginning of the day you will cover Module 2a.

☐ Post the Facts and Message for Module 2b at your classroom Message Station at the beginning of the day you will cover Module 2b.

Everyone everywhere has the same needs.

Vocabulary for Power 2

(These words are used in Modules 2a and 2b and in following modules. You may want to review these terms with your students before or during the modules.)

- thrive
- explore
- needs
- Human Needs

- universal
- Universal Human Needs
- Surviving Needs
- Thriving Needs

Module 2a: Universal Needs

Objective: To increase self-awareness and awareness of others by recognizing human needs for surviving and for thriving and noticing that everyone has the same needs

Activities:

☐ Volunteers read Notes from the No-Fault Zone, Facts and Message (15 minutes)

☐ Exploration: *Universal Human Needs List* (45 minutes)

Type of Activity: Teacher-led discussion

Materials:

☑ Materials to prepare in advance: None

Materials for construction:

☐ Chart paper

☐ Easel or blue tape

☐ Markers

Materials to be constructed in class during Module 2a:

☐ Universal Human Needs List

Materials constructed previously to be used in Module 2a:

☐ IOS Power Panels, Choice Cards, tokens for Feeling Thermometers

As you learn more about your needs, you will have more and more Power to take good care of you.

Module 2b: The #1 Activity on Planet Earth

Objective: To add to a vocabulary of needs; to learn to look for the needs behind everything people do and say

Activities:

☐ Volunteers read Notes from the No-Fault Zone, Facts and Message (15 minutes)

☐ Exploration: *Needs Card Deck* (45 minutes)

Type of Activity: Construction

☐ Follow-on Exploration: *Motivation for Action* (15-minute optional exercise for a different day than the day you do Module 2b)

Type of Activity: Game

Materials:

✔ Materials to prepare in advance: None

Materials for construction:

☐ Blank yellow 3" x 5" index cards (5 per student plus extras)

☐ Pens or markers

☐ Scissors

☐ Rubber bands (1 per student)

Materials to be constructed in class during Module 2b:

☐ Needs Card Decks

Materials constructed previously to be used in Module 2b:

☐ IOS Power Panels, Choice Cards, Universal Human Needs List

Get to know your needs.

Module 2a: Universal Needs

Notes from the No-Fault Zone

Michi: Hi everyone! Nao and I are excited to start talking about Power 2: The Power to Know What You Need. There's a lot to explore, and you will be making and collecting a lot of new Power cards starting today. But first, we'd like to make sure that you all have your materials: your IOS Power Panel and your Energy-Shift Choice Card. You can raise your Energy-Shift Choice Card to let us know that you're ready to listen to what's next.

[PAUSE until everyone has their Choice Card and Power Panel out.]

Nao: So, the Power cards you will start collecting today are called Need Cards. Needs are ... well, they are all the things you and everyone else on planet Earth must have to survive and to thrive.

Michi: Yes, so some needs you know about are food and water and sleep.

Nao: Other needs are friends and learning and play.

Michi: And there's a bunch more to learn about.

Nao: As you learn more about your needs, you will have more and more Power to take care of them, and to take good care of you.

Michi: Learning how many needs there are and noticing them in your IOS is a place to start.

Nao: And did we say that everyone everywhere has the same needs? This is an important fact to remember for constructing a No-Fault Zone in your classroom, at home and out in the world.

Michi: But don't take our word for it. Check it out for yourself.

POWER 2a

FACTS

◉ The well-being of Earthlings depends on learning how to meet needs.

◉ If they choose, Earthlings can develop skills for meeting needs.

◉ Earthlings have Surviving Needs (like air, water, food, shelter and safety) and Thriving Needs (things that make life wonderful like friends, family, learning, play, respect, kindness and many more).

◉ All Earthlings are born with and operate from the *same* set of Human Needs.

POWER 2a

MESSAGE

⊙ Get to know your needs—your Surviving Needs and your Thriving Needs—so you can meet them well.

⊙ Notice that everyone operates from the same Human Needs.

Exploration: *Universal Human Needs List* (45 minutes)

Objective: To meet needs for learning; to identify Universal Human Needs; to expand needs vocabulary; to differentiate between needs and strategies

Materials: IOS Power Panels, tokens for Feeling Thermometer, chart paper, easel or blue tape, markers

Type of Activity: Teacher-led discussion

Procedure:

1. Get to Calm Alert: Ask students to take a Feeling Thermometer read-out. If needed, ask a student to lead an Energy-Shifting exercise so students can get to Calm Alert for this activity. (You can allow up to 20 minutes for this if you like: the more time it takes to get to Calm Alert, the less you will have for your discussion and list.)

2. Begin a class discussion: *The Twins say that everyone on Earth has the same needs. Is this true?*

3. Encourage students to respond.

4. Title a new page of chart paper "**Universal Human Needs**" and post it on the wall.

5. Teacher: *Let's see if we can discover: what are the Universal Human Needs?*

7. List responses on the chart paper. (See below for tips on distinguishing needs from strategies. Write up only the needs on the Universal Human Needs List.)

8. Post the list of Universal Human Needs in a place where all students can see it.

Tips to Distinguish Needs from Strategies:

Needs are distinct from strategies: computers are *ways* to meet needs, not needs. When students suggest strategies rather than needs, try this approach to come up with needs instead:

Ask: *Does everyone on earth need _____?*

If yes, it is a need.

If no, ask:

> *What needs do <u>cars</u> meet?* Transportation, getting from place to place
>
> *What need does <u>money</u> meet?* Mutual exchange
>
> *What needs do <u>video games</u> meet?* Entertainment, fun, play
>
> *What needs do <u>computers</u> meet?* Tool for work, communication, entertainment, creativity

Supporting Activities

- Teacher Practice: Develop your needs vocabulary; Distinguish between a need and a strategy.

- Add to the Universal Human Needs List throughout the week and year.

- Practice Energy-Shifting exercises that have been introduced and introduce new ones.

- Review your class's Group Agreements: Ask, How are they working?

Module 2b: The #1 Activity on Planet Earth

Notes from the No-Fault Zone

Nao: Have you ever been puzzled by what someone else does?

Michi: Yeah, like when your mom, or dad, or friend suddenly gets red in the face and angry and you wonder what it's all about?

Nao: Or maybe it's something you did or said and you wonder why you did it, because it made things worse for you, not better.

Michi: Today we're going to explore what's behind everything we do, and everything other people do: our values and our needs.

Nao: Seeing the reasons why we do what we do can be very interesting, and even solve some mysteries. It is definitely helpful for building a No-Fault Zone.

Michi: Check it out for yourself!

POWER 2b

FACTS

⦾ There is a need behind every action.

⦾ Most Earthlings don't know this.

⦾ When Earthlings understand why they do what they do, they can be more effective, create more understanding and decrease conflicts.

POWER 2b

MESSAGE

◉ Add to your vocabulary of needs.

◉ Look for the need behind everything you do and say, and everything other people do and say, and see what you can learn from that.

Exploration: *Needs Card Deck* (45 minutes)

Objective: To create a tool for communication and conflict resolution; to add to and practice a needs vocabulary

Materials: Yellow 3" x 5" index cards (5 per student), scissors to cut them in two, pens or markers, rubber band for each student to keep their Need Cards together, Universal Human Needs List (post in front of classroom so all can see)

Type of Activity: Construction

Procedure:

1. Hand out yellow index cards, five per student.

2. Ask students to cut them in half lengthwise to make ten yellow 3" x 2.5" cards.

3. Ask students to write one need that is important to them on each of their ten cards.

4. Tell students they can walk around the room to get ideas from other students about their most important needs. Have extra blank yellow index cards available in case some students want to make more than ten today, as well as for future weeks.*

---

*Note: Some students may want additional time during the week to work on their Card Decks—free time, breaks, before or after school or an additional class period. Have blank cards and markers available in the No-Fault Construction Zone for these times.

Supporting Activities

- Teacher Practice: Make your own Needs Card Deck. Keep it at your desk to use and continue to add to it.

- Ask students to add to their decks until they have fifteen or more cards. These cards will be used throughout the Explorations in future modules.

- Show of Cards: If students are acting restless, ask students to hold up the Need Card that expresses what's up for them.

- Ask for volunteers to make two larger decks of cards (one 3" x 5" yellow index card for each Need Card) to use for classroom demonstrations.

Curricular Tie-ins

In your studies of history, science, social studies, literature:

Select figures from literature, history, social studies or science and ask: *What need was this person or group of people trying to meet by their actions?* You can ask students to make their guesses* out loud or to select and show one or more of their Need Cards.

*Note: When making guesses about the needs behind actions of actual living people, remember that you are always and only guessing. It is important to check it out with the person to find out if a guess is accurate.

Follow-on Exploration: *Motivation for Action*

Objective: To recognize the needs behind every action

Materials: Small (2" x 5") slips of paper, a paper bag, a deck of Need Cards (preferably a large classroom deck that all can see)

Type of Activity: Game

Procedure:

1. Tell your class that the purpose is to explore this statement: "Everything we do is an attempt to meet a need."

2. Ask students to write, on a small slip of paper, one thing they did this morning before coming to school.

3. Fold the papers and put them in a paper bag (or hat or bowl).

4. Ask one student to draw a slip of paper from the bag and read it.

5. Ask your class: *What need was this person trying to meet when they did that?*

6. Ask the student who read the paper to choose a Need Card from the Needs Card Deck.

7. If students are unsure about which needs are trying to be met, look together at the Universal Human Needs List and determine a list of possibilities. You can check with the student who wrote it to see if she or he agrees with the need chosen.

8. Have students take turns and continue to draw slips of paper and select Need Cards.

9. Ask your class: *Can you think of anything you have done that wasn't an attempt to meet one of the Universal Human Needs?*

10. Encourage students to continue to look for a human action that doesn't meet a universal need. Keep a list of ideas for discussion.

POWER 3 ▪ **The Power to Meet Needs**

TEACHER PREPARATION

Advance Preparation for Modules 3a and 3b

☐ Assemble the materials required for each module (see Materials lists on the pages that follow).

☐ Photocopy the Notes from the No-Fault Zone narrative script from both modules for two to four student readers.

☐ Photocopy the Facts and Message for both modules.

☐ Post the Facts and Message for Module 3a at your classroom Message Station at the beginning of the day you will cover Module 3a.

☐ Post the Facts and Message for Module 3b at your classroom Message Station at the beginning of the day you will cover Module 3b.

Vocabulary for Power 3

(These words are used in Modules 3a and 3b and in following modules. You may want to review these terms with your students before or during the modules.)

- ◉ meet needs
- ◉ requests
- ◉ stress
- ◉ short circuit
- ◉ strategies
- ◉ inventor
- ◉ experiment
- ◉ mis-take
- ◉ scientists

Module 3a: Many Ways to Meet Needs

Objective: To discover many ways to meet needs; to expand students' range of choices for how to meet needs

Activities:

❑ Volunteers read Notes from the No-Fault Zone, Facts and Message (15 minutes)

❑ Exploration: *Many Ways to Meet Needs* (45 minutes)

Type of Activity: Small-group charting

Materials:

Materials to prepare in advance:

❑ Prep blank Many Ways to Meet Needs charts (see Exploration: *Many Ways to Meet Needs*)

Materials for construction:

❑ Chart paper

❑ Markers

Materials to be constructed in class during Module 3a:

❑ Many Ways to Meet Needs charts

✔ Materials constructed previously to be used in Module 3a: None

Who's in charge of meeting your needs?

Module 3b: Learn from Successes & Mis-takes

Objective: To learn from real-life experiments; to proceed with the curiosity of a scientist and reflect on these questions: What did I do? What was the result? What needs were met? What needs weren't met? What would I do differently next time?

Activities:

☐ Volunteers read Notes from the No-Fault Zone, Facts and Message (15 minutes)

☐ Exploration: *Learn from Real-Life Experiments* (45 minutes)

Type of Activity: Small-group exercise

Materials:

Materials to prepare in advance:

☐ Photocopies of the Real-Life Experiment Log (see Appendix 2), enough for each student and for stock in the No-Fault Construction Zone

Materials for construction:

☐ Drawing paper

☐ Crayons, colored pencils

☐ Blank yellow 3" x 5" index cards (for additions to Needs Card Decks)

☐ Scissors

Materials to be constructed in class during Module 3b:

☐ Additional Need Cards

Materials constructed previously to be used in Module 3b:

☐ Needs Card Decks, Universal Human Needs List (to be visible on wall)

Module 3a: Many Ways to Meet Needs

Notes from the No-Fault Zone

Nao: Today's Exploration is all about finding the best ways to meet your needs. This will add a lot to your Powers.

Michi: Before we begin, let's do a Power check. Make sure you all have your IOS Power Panel, your Energy-Shift Choice Card and your Need Cards. You may not need them all today, but it's good to have them available. You can raise your Energy-Shift Choice Card to let us know you're ready.

[PAUSE here to make sure everyone has these materials.]

Nao: Okay then, we start with a question: Who's in charge of meeting your needs?

Think about it for a moment. Growing up is all about taking charge of meeting your own needs. When you were a baby you needed lots and lots of help. And you still do need help from parents and friends. Even adults ask for help from other people.

Michi: So it's not about not asking for help. It's about knowing what you need so you can tell other people what it is you'd like help with. Making clear requests of others will help you a lot.

Nao: For example, if you really want someone to listen, but you don't tell anyone, how will they know? Or if you yell at them instead of saying you want them to listen, they probably won't get the real message, or want to help.

Michi: Today we explore ways to meet your needs.

Nao: The first thing is to know that there are lots of ways to meet needs. If one person isn't able to listen to me, I can find someone else who can listen.

Michi: Yeah, and if you are feeling restless in class, but it's not time for recess, you could try an Energy Shifter to see if you can get to Calm Alert, or try something else.

Nao: When I know there are many ways to meet needs I don't feel so frustrated or stuck if something doesn't work out the way I wanted. I know there are more ways than one.

Michi: But don't just take our word for it. See how many ways you can find to meet your needs, in the Exploration ahead. And in your life.

POWER 3a

FACTS

◉ The well-being of Earthlings depends on seeing more than one way to meet a need.

◉ There are many ways to meet needs!

◉ When Earthlings see just one way to meet a need, they feel stress and short-circuit their power.

◉ When Earthlings see many ways to meet a need, they relax and can trust they will find a way that is satisfying.

◉ If they choose, Earthlings can learn to see many ways to meet a need.

POWER 3a

MESSAGE

◉ Explore the Power you have to find many ways to meet your needs.

Exploration: *Many Ways to Meet Needs* (45 minutes)

Objective: To get to know each other; to discover many ways to meet needs; to expand students' range of choices for how to meet needs

Materials: Chart paper, markers

Type of Activity: Small-group charting

Procedure:

1. Introduce today's Exploration: *Today's exploration is about how we meet needs.*

2. Divide the class into groups of 4–5. (For very young students, this can be a class activity instead, with the teacher leading the discussion and writing the student responses.)

3. Give each group one piece of chart paper* with one of the following needs written in large clear letters at the top: Play, Respect, Learning, Fun, Safety, Peace, Exercise.

4. Ask each student in the group to write on the chart one way they meet the need at the top of their paper and put their name next to what they write.

5. When all groups have finished with their own chart, ask students to move as a group to another chart, add one strategy each and write their names next to what they write. Continue in this way until all students have written on all of the charts. Post the charts in the classroom.

6. Look at each chart and ask: *What do you notice?* and *What was your experience doing this Exploration?*

*Note: You can prepare the charts ahead of time by making lines across the chart so each student writes on one line, or they can be designed in other ways by you or by the students.

Growing up is all about taking charge of meeting your own needs.

Supporting Activities

- Teacher Practice: Notice the strategies you most often use for meeting your needs. Think up some new ones you could try.

- Use Energy-Shifting exercises with your class, as needed.

- Continue to add to Needs Card Decks.

- Make new charts for the Exploration: Many Ways to Meet Needs as new needs come up in class.

Curricular Tie-ins

In your studies of history, science, social studies, literature:

Look at both the needs people had and the strategies they chose to meet them. Discuss with students:

- *What need was calling attention to itself?*

- *What strategy did people choose to meet that need?*

- *What was the result?*

- *Can you think of other strategies they might have used for different results?*

Module 3b: Learn from Successes & Mis-takes

Notes from the No-Fault Zone

Nao: Do you know that the great inventor Thomas Edison tried thousands of different experiments before he finally discovered how electricity works? He said, "If I find ten thousand ways something won't work, I haven't failed." That's because he was always learning something new that helped him figure out what *would* work.

Michi: Earthling scientists are trained in school to learn something from every experiment. I wish all Earthlings were trained that way so they didn't waste time feeling bad or saying they failed or they "blew it" when they just make a mis-take. Mis-takes are part of trying new things.

Nao: Right. You can learn from successes and also from mis-takes, and have more fun that way.

Michi: If you sometimes feel bad about yourself when you make a mis-take, we hope you'll see another way soon, to be kinder to yourself and have more fun learning.

POWER 3b

FACTS

⊙ Life on Earth is made up of one experiment after another.

⊙ Earthlings can learn from experiments what works best to meet needs.

⊙ Earthlings stop learning from their experiments when they see mis-takes as failures.

⊙ Earthlings can learn from what their scientists know: not to judge any experiment as a failure but see what they can learn from it.

POWER 3b

MESSAGE

◉ To learn from your real-life experiments, proceed with the curiosity of a scientist and reflect on these questions:

1. What did I do?

2. What was the result?

3. What needs were met?

4. What needs weren't met?

5. What would I do differently next time?

Exploration: *Learn from Real-Life Experiments* (45 minutes)

Objective: To discover the numerous ways there are to meet needs; to learn from the results of your real-life experiments

Materials: Drawing paper, crayons, colored pencils, Needs Card Decks, copies of the Real-Life Experiment Log (see Appendix 2)

Type of Activity: Small-group exercise

Procedure:

1. Introduce today's Exploration: *Today we're going to explore how to learn the most from real-life experiments.*

2. Ask students each to write or draw about something they did recently that didn't turn out the way they wanted.

3. When they have finished, ask them to get into small groups of 2–4 and reflect on these questions:

   What did you do? (What was your strategy?)

   What was the result?

   What needs did it meet?

4. Ask students to find the Need Card(s) from their Card Deck that represent what needs were met and place it in front of them. If they're not sure they've found the need, they can ask their group or the class for help. If they don't have the Need Card they want, they can make it to add to their Needs Card Deck.

5. Ask students to discuss in their small groups: Were there any needs that their strategy didn't meet?

6. Ask students to think of three other strategies they might have tried. (Students can share answers with the group or in their dyads or triads.)

7. Introduce students to the Real-Life Experiment Log. Some may want to fill a log out for this Exploration. They can use the log whenever they want to sort out situations in their life. Keep a stack of Real-Life Experiment Logs in your No-Fault Construction Zone for students to use.

> Mis-takes are part of trying new things.

Supporting Activities

- Teacher Practice: Notice your reactions when you make a mis-take. See if the reflection questions in the Message for Module 3b or filling out the Real-Life Experiment Log help you learn from your mis-takes, without judging or blaming.

- Keep copies of the Real-Life Experiment Log in your No-Fault Construction Zone. When a student does something that doesn't work out the way they want, suggest they fill out a Real-Life Experiment Log to help them learn from mis-takes and avoid judging themselves or their experiment as a failure.

Curricular Tie-ins

In your studies of literature and history:

Discuss together actions people have taken (both fictional characters in literature and historical characters) using these exploratory questions:

- *What need do you think they were trying to meet?*

- *What strategy did they choose?*

- *What was the result?*

- *Was it successful at meeting their needs?*

- *Did their actions get in the way of other people (or animals or the environment) meeting their needs?*

If there was conflict or if there were unhappy results from the actions that were chosen, ask:

- *Can you think of other strategies they could have used that might have had better results?*

POWER 4 ▪ **The Power to Read Feelings**

TEACHER PREPARATION

Advance Preparation for Modules 4a and 4b

- ☐ Assemble the materials required for each module (see Materials lists on the pages that follow).

- ☐ Photocopy the Notes from the No-Fault Zone narrative script from both modules for two to four student readers.

- ☐ Photocopy the Facts and Message for both modules.

- ☐ Post the Facts and Message for Module 4a at your classroom Message Station at the beginning of the day you will cover Module 4a.

- ☐ Post the Facts and Message for Module 4b at your classroom Message Station at the beginning of the day you will cover Module 4b.

You can "read" your Feelings.

Vocabulary for Power 4

(These words are used in Modules 4a and 4b and in following modules. You may want to review these terms with your students before or during the modules.)

- ⊙ feelings
- ⊙ signals
- ⊙ vital
- ⊙ detect

- ⊙ detective
- ⊙ judgments
- ⊙ opinions
- ⊙ interpretations

Module 4a: The Feeling-Need Connection

Objective: To create a tool for understanding, communication and conflict resolution; to add to and practice a feelings vocabulary; to recognize that feelings and needs are connected

Activities:

- ❏ Volunteers read Notes from the No-Fault Zone, Facts and Message (15 minutes)

- ❏ Exploration: *The Connection Between Feelings & Needs* (5 minutes)

    Type of Activity: Class discussion

- ❏ Exploration: *Inventory Feelings* (15 minutes)

    Type of Activity: Class discussion

- ❏ Exploration: *Make Feelings Card Decks* (25 minutes)

    Type of Activity: Construction

- ❏ Follow-on Exploration: *Guess the Feeling* (5- to 20-minute optional exercise for a different day than the day you do Module 4a)

    Type of Activity: Pantomime

Feelings are always sending signals to "Pay Attention to needs!"

Materials:

Materials to prepare in advance:

- ❏ Blank Feelings List (see Exploration: *Inventory Feelings*)

Materials for construction:

- ❏ Chart paper
- ❏ Easel or blue tape
- ❏ Markers
- ❏ Pink 3" x 5" index cards (5–10 per student, plus extras)
- ❏ Scissors
- ❏ Pens

Materials to be constructed in class during Module 4a:

- ☐ Feelings List

- ☐ Feelings Card Decks

- ☐ Large Feelings Card Deck for classroom demonstrations

Materials constructed previously to be used in Module 4a:

- ☐ IOS Power Panels, tokens for Feeling Thermometer, Energy-Shift Choice Card, Need Cards

Materials to be used in the Follow-on Exploration:

- ☐ A deck of Feeling Cards (preferably a large classroom deck that all can see)

Module 4b: Feelings vs Thoughts

Objective: To prevent confusion, misunderstanding and conflict by learning to detect the difference between feelings and thoughts and describe feelings in a way that keeps them separate from thoughts

Earthlings often confuse feelings and thoughts.

Activities:

- ☐ Volunteers read Notes from the No-Fault Zone, Facts and Message (15 minutes)

- ☐ Exploration: *How to Tell a Feeling from a Thought* (25 minutes)

  Type of Activity: Teacher-led discussion

- ☐ Exploration: *Fake Feelings—More Ways Thoughts and Feelings Get Mixed Together* (20 minutes)

  Type of Activity: Construction, class discussion

- ☐ Follow-on Exploration: *Don't Give Others Power Over Your Feelings* (15 minute optional exercise for a different day than the day you do Module 4b)

  Type of Activity: Class discussion

Materials:

Materials to prepare in advance:

◻ Small slips of paper with Feeling & Thought Statements written on them (if using the variation to Exploration: *How to Tell a Feeling from a Thought*)

◻ Paper bag, hat or box (if using the variation to Exploration: *How to Tell a Feeling from a Thought*)

Materials for construction:

◻ Chart paper

◻ Markers

◻ White 3" x 5" index cards (2 per student)

Materials to be constructed in class during Module 4b:

◻ List of Feeling Statements

◻ List of Thought Statements

◻ "Feeling" and "Thought" flash cards

Materials constructed previously to be used in Module 4b:

◻ IOS Power Panels, tokens for Feeling Thermometer

✔ Materials to be used in the Follow-on Exploration: None

Module 4a: The Feeling–Need Connection

Notes from the No-Fault Zone

Michi: We have fun places to explore today. First, a Power check: Make sure you have your IOS Power Panel, your Need Cards, and your Energy-Shift Choice Card. You can raise your Choice Card to let us know you're ready.

[PAUSE to make sure everyone has their materials.]

Nao: Today we're exploring a new area of your IOS: feelings. Knowing your feelings is very important to your well-being, and you can learn to take a read-out of your feelings whenever you want to see what's going on inside. To help you do this, you will start a Feelings Card Deck today.

Michi: Most Earthlings know a few of their feelings, like happy, sad, mad, scared, surprised. But there are lots more feelings to learn how to "read" once you know where to look.

Nao: We think you'll have fun seeing the number of feelings there are in your Internal Operating System. You may be surprised to count how many of them come up in a day, or in an hour or even in a few minutes.

Michi: Not many Earthlings ask, "where do feelings come from?" And not many know the answer. What we know in the No-Fault Zone is that feelings are connected to needs. They're helpful signals, like the red lights on the dashboard of the car saying, "Pay Attention!"

Nao: Or like a telephone ringing saying, "Pay Attention! Needs are calling!"

Michi: Just think: How would you know that your body needs food if you didn't have feelings of hunger, like a growling stomach, to tell you? All uncomfortable feelings send a signal in your IOS for you to take care of some need, or a few different needs.

Nao: And comfortable, happy feelings send a signal that a need is taken care of. That's something to celebrate! Feelings are always sending you signals to "Pay Attention!"

Michi: I'm feeling very curious right now to see what you discover about feelings in the next two Explorations. So let's go!

POWER 4a

FACTS

⊚ The well-being of Earthlings depends on getting an accurate read-out of feelings.

⊚ Feelings give Earthlings information about their needs.

⊚ When needs are being met, Earthlings have feelings like calm, peaceful, satisfied and content. When needs are not being met, Earthlings have feelings like sad, mad, frustrated and afraid.

⊚ If they choose, Earthlings can learn to "read" what their feelings are and learn how to work with them.

POWER 4a

MESSAGE

- ◉ Develop your feeling vocabulary.

- ◉ Get to know your feelings. They are sending vital messages about what's important to you and what you need.

Exploration: *The Connection Between Feelings & Needs*
(5 minutes)

Objective: To explore the connection between feelings and needs

Materials: IOS Power Panels, tokens for Feeling Thermometer

Type of Activity: Class discussion

Procedure:

1. Get to Calm Alert: Ask students to take a Feeling Thermometer read-out. If needed, ask a student to lead an Energy-Shifting exercise so students can get to Calm Alert for this activity.

2. Begin Discussion: Reiterate the Twins' message:

    All feelings are helpful, alerting us to what we need. For example, if we haven't eaten in a long while, feeling hungry or irritable signals it's time for us to eat. At the end of the day, feeling tired and grumpy tells us it's time to sleep. All feelings are helpful signals of our needs.

3. Ask students this question and listen to their responses: *Think of a time when you hadn't eaten a meal for a long time, you felt hungry and then you ate. How did you feel?*

4. Ask students this question and listen to their responses: *Think of a time when you wanted understanding and you got it. How did you feel?*

5. Ask students this question and listen to their responses: *Think of a time when you wanted understanding and you didn't get it. How did you feel?*

6. Ask students: *Do you have any questions about feelings?*

7. Proceed to the next Exploration: *Inventory Feelings.*

Exploration: *Inventory Feelings* (15 minutes)

Objective: To connect feelings to needs; to expand students' feeling vocabulary

Materials: Chart paper (1 piece), easel or blue tape, markers

Type of Activity: Class discussion

Procedure:

1. Make two columns on a large page of chart paper. At the top of the page write the title: "**FEELINGS**." At the top of Column 1 write: "**When Needs Are Met**." At the top of Column 2 write: "**When Needs Are Not Met**."

2. As a group, encourage students to think of all the feelings they can and decide if each one fits into either Column 1 or Column 2. Write the feelings on the list in Column 1 or Column 2 (or both).

3. Proceed to the next Exploration: *Make Feelings Card Decks*.

Exploration: *Make Feelings Card Decks* (25 minutes)

Objective: To create a tool for understanding, communication and conflict resolution; to add to and practice feelings vocabulary; to recognize that feelings and needs are connected

Materials: Pink 3" x 5" index cards (5–10 cards per student), scissors, pens or markers, Feelings List (posted in front of classroom so all can see)

Type of Activity: Construction

Procedure:

1. Hand out 5–10 pink index cards to each student and ask them to cut their cards in half lengthwise so they have 10–20 Feeling Cards.

2. Ask students to write one feeling on each card. Students can refer to the Feelings List on the wall or walk around the room to get ideas from other students.

3. Students may need additional time during the week to work on their Card Decks—during free time, breaks, before or after school or during any additional class period used for *No-Fault Classroom* activities. Keep a stock of blank cards and markers available in the No-Fault Construction Zone.

Supporting Activities

- Teacher Practice: Make your own Feelings Card Deck.

- Photocopy The Feelings & Needs Connection worksheet from Appendix 2 and keep a stack in the No-Fault Construction Zone for students to use as needed.

- Ask students to add to their Feelings Card Deck until they have 15 or more cards.These cards will be used in Explorations to come.

- When a new feeling word is introduced in class, add the word to your class Feelings List. Students can then add it to their Feelings Card Deck as well.

- Ask for volunteers to make two larger decks of cards (one 3" x 5" pink index card for each Feeling Card) to use for classroom demonstrations.

- Ask for a Brief Show of Cards: When students act restless, ask them to hold up the Feeling Cards and/or Need Cards that express what's up for them.

Curricular Tie-ins

In your studies of history, science, social studies, literature:

Select figures from literature, history, social studies or science and ask: *What was this person (or group of people) feeling when they did what they did?* What need did they want to meet? You can ask students to make their guesses* out loud or to select and show one or more of their Feeling and Need Cards.

> *Note: When making guesses about the needs behind the actions of actual living people, remember (and remind students) that you are always and only guessing. It is important to check it out with the person to find out if a guess is accurate.

You can also use the Card Decks to discuss different sides in scientific, political, historical or other debates. One, two or more students can represent a side. Ask students to use Feeling Cards to show what feelings people on each side of the debate have and Need Cards to show the needs at the root of those feelings.

Follow-on Exploration: *Guess the Feeling*
(5 to 20 minutes as desired)

Objective: To identify feelings by using facial and body cues; to have fun

Materials: A large Feelings Card Deck, big enough for everyone to read

Type of Activity: Pantomime

Procedure:

1. Ask a student volunteer to stand up (either inside a circle or at the front of the room).

2. Ask the student to cut the deck of Feeling Cards and show one card to the class without looking at it.

3. Ask the student who has not seen the card to call on another student to act out the feeling. The goal is for the standing student to guess the feeling that's on the card.

4. Other students may want to take turns and get a chance to be the guesser, depending on the amount of time set aside for the activity.

Variation: *Feeling Charades*

One person selects a Feeling Card and reads it silently but doesn't show it to anyone else. That person then acts out the feeling, and the other students call out their guesses (or are called on individually to make a guess).

Both Explorations, *Guess the Feeling* and *Feeling Charades*, are activities that can be repeated in short sessions throughout the week and at other times for energy, for fun and to build students' feeling vocabulary.

Module 4b: Feelings vs Thoughts

Notes from the No-Fault Zone

Nao: Since feelings are such important signals in your IOS, it's important you get a clear read-out. A clear read-out is usually short. It might sound like this: I feel sad. I feel scared. I feel happy.

Michi: The tricky part is that Earthlings often mix up their feelings with their thoughts. When they do, it can cause a lot of confusion and misunderstandings. Like someone might say, "I feel that she doesn't want to play with me." You notice that this doesn't tell you the speaker's feeling? It tells you her thought instead: she is *thinking* that the other person doesn't want to play with her.

Nao: When someone mixes up feelings and thoughts like this, you might have to do some detective work to guess their feeling. I guess this person's feeling is sad, hurt or disappointed.

Michi: You can train yourself to think like a detective and detect the difference between a feeling and a thought. This is what you'll be practicing in today's Explorations. Have fun!

POWER 4b

FACTS

⊙ Earthlings often confuse feelings and thoughts. Many times they say **I feel** when they really mean **I think**.

⊙ Mixing in thoughts with feelings contributes to confusion, misunderstandings and conflict.

POWER 4b

MESSAGE

⊙ To prevent confusion and conflict, make sure that when you describe your feelings, you keep them separate from your thoughts.

Exploration: *How to Tell a Feeling from a Thought*
(25 minutes)

Objective: To learn to differentiate between feelings and thoughts

Materials: IOS Power Panels, tokens for Feeling Thermometer, List of Feeling & Thought Statements (provided on the next page, following the procedures), chart paper, markers

Type of Activity: Teacher-led discussion

Procedure:

1. Get to Calm Alert: Ask students to take a Feeling Thermometer read-out. If needed, ask a student to lead an Energy-Shifting exercise so students can get to Calm Alert for this activity.

2. Reiterate Twins' Message: *Feelings result when needs are met and when they are not met. Feelings are usually just one word: sad, mad, glad, upset, worried and so forth, and they can be expressed in three words: I feel mad. I feel sad. I feel happy.*

   Thoughts are ideas, opinions, judgments or interpretations. Thoughts are often expressed in the following ways:

   "I think *that* it's unfair."

   "I think *that* she doesn't work hard enough."

   "I think *that* she is mean."

   Earthlings sometimes confuse feelings and thoughts and use the word "feel" to express a thought, as in the following sentences:

   "I feel *that* it's unfair."

   "I feel *that* she doesn't work hard enough."

   "I feel *that* she's mean."

   In fact, when Earthlings say the word that, *it is almost always followed by a thought and not a feeling.*

3. Read the Feeling & Thought Statements below, and after each statement ask students to raise their hands to determine who thinks the statement is a feeling and who thinks it is a thought.

4. Ask each group of students to give their reasons for their choice. Help clarify the distinction between feelings and thoughts when necessary.

5. Ask students to write their own feeling and thought statements. They can read their statement out loud and have other students guess whether it is a feeling or a thought.

6. At the end of the Exploration, ask for volunteers to gather all statements and write them in two columns on chart paper: one page titled "**Feelings**," and one titled "**Thoughts**." Post the lists in the classroom and add to them regularly.

Feeling & Thought Statements

"I feel impatient." (feeling)

"I feel excited." (feeling)

"I feel that you shouldn't tease me." (thought)

"I feel that he's mean." (thought)

"I feel very relaxed." (feeling)

"I feel I blew it." (thought)

"I'm furious." (feeling)

"I feel peaceful." (feeling)

"I feel you are irritating." (thought)

"I'm concerned." (feeling)

"I feel that you should be more considerate." (thought)

"I feel upset." (feeling)

"I feel excited." (feeling)

"I feel hopeful." (feeling)

"I feel like something needs to change or I quit." (thought)

"I feel like you should be more understanding." (thought)

"I feel that you are bossy." (thought)

"I feel amazed." (feeling)

"I feel that there is too much noise in here." (thought)

"I feel that you are rushing me." (thought)

Variation: *Feeling* or *Thought*?

Write feeling and thought statements on individual slips of paper and put them in a paper bag. Ask students to choose one, read it aloud and say whether it is a feeling or thought. They can confer with someone if they are confused.

Go on to the next Exploration: *Fake Feelings—More Ways Thoughts & Feelings Get Mixed Together*

Exploration: *Fake Feelings—More Ways Thoughts & Feelings Get Mixed Together* (20 minutes)

Objective: To learn to recognize the difference between feelings and thoughts mistaken for feelings

Materials: White 3" x 5" index cards (2 per student), pens or markers

Type of Activity: Construction, class discussion

Procedure:

Remember to think like a detective.

1. Give each student two 3" x 5" index cards. Ask them to write "**Feeling**" on one and "**Thought**" on the other.

2. Explain: *Feelings are signals in your IOS. Feelings are your body signals about what is going on. Expressions of feelings sound like this: I feel sad. I feel worried. I feel scared. I feel excited.*

3. Explain: *Thoughts are your ideas about what you or others are doing. For example: I think you are trying to control me. I think you aren't listening to me.*

4. Explain: *People often mix up feelings and thoughts and say things like this: I feel controlled. I feel ignored.*

5. Give instructions: *In the following sentences, listen for the difference between expressions of feelings and expressions of thoughts or ideas about what others are doing. Hold up your "Feeling" card when you hear a feeling. Hold up your "Thought" card when you hear a thought.*

6. Teacher reads a statement from the list below: *"I feel ignored."*

7. All students hold up either their "**Feeling**" or "**Thought**" card.

8. Select a student who has raised the thought card.

9. Discuss: *Yes, "I feel ignored" is a thought, not a feeling. What thought is behind this statement?* (Example: I think that you are ignoring me.) If the student you ask is unsure what thought is behind the statement, they can ask for help from another student.

10. Review: Read the same statement again (*I feel ignored.*) and explain how to discover the feeling behind the thought, which is to ask: *How do you feel when you think you are being ignored?* (Some possible feelings: hurt, surprised, relieved, etc.)

11. Repeat steps 6 through 10: Read another statement from the list below, or ask a student to read a statement. Repeat all steps 7 through 10 for statements that are disguised "thought" statements. If the statement expresses a real feeling rather than a fake feeling, agree that it is a feeling and move on to the next statement.

More Feeling & Thought Statements

"I'm upset." (feeling)

"I feel cornered." (thought)

"I feel controlled." (thought)

"I feel hungry." (feeling)

"I feel left out." (thought)

"I feel put down." (thought)

"I feel rejected." (thought)

"I feel relaxed." (feeling)

"I feel tricked." (thought)

"I feel abandoned." (thought)

"I feel concerned." (feeling)

"I feel attacked." (thought)

"I feel scared." (feeling)

"I feel blamed." (thought)

Fake Feelings: Words that Disguise Thoughts as Feelings

(Read this list of Fake Feelings to students and post it in the classroom so students can add to it.)

- accepted
- criticized
- disrespected
- dissed
- dumped on
- hassled
- ignored
- insulted
- intimidated
- invalidated
- left out
- manipulated
- misunderstood

- neglected
- patronized
- pressured
- put down
- rejected
- ripped off
- smothered
- threatened
- trapped
- unheard
- unimportant
- unseen
- used

Supporting Activities

- Teacher Practice: Notice when you mix up feelings and thoughts in your thinking and speaking.

- During the week, students can collect the feeling statements and feeling statements mixed with thoughts that they hear. They can list their collected statements on chart paper. They can also list the fake feeling statements they hear.

- Ask students to complete the Feelings vs Thoughts worksheet. (Worksheet found in Appendix 2, although you may have already provided photocopies in the No-Fault Construction Zone as suggested in Module 4a. Answer Key to Feelings vs Thoughts worksheet: F T F F T T F F T F T T T F T T F T T T.)

- Notice opportunities to ask students to fill out Real-Life Experiment Logs.

Curricular Tie-ins

In your studies of literature:

When reading dialogue in stories, watch for instances when characters use fake feelings.

Follow-on Exploration: *Don't Give Others Power Over Your Feelings* (15 minutes)

Objective: To learn how to take responsibility for feelings

Materials: None

Type of Activity: Class discussion

Procedure:

1. Get to Calm Alert: Ask students to take a Feeling Thermometer read-out. If needed, ask a student to lead an Energy-Shifting exercise so students can get to Calm Alert for this activity.

2. Give information: *Feelings are signals telling us about needs. Your feelings are yours and other people don't have power over them—unless you give it to them.*

    You give others power over your feelings when you say things like this:

    > "You make me happy."

    > "She makes me mad."

    > "He annoys me."

    These statements say that what others do has the power to make you happy, mad or annoyed. This makes others responsible for how you feel because you see them as the cause of how you feel.

    When you make statements that connect your feelings with your needs, you take responsibility for what is happening in your IOS. Here's what this might sound like:

    > "I feel happy when you ask how my day is going. It meets my need for friendship and kindness."

    > "I feel mad when I see him take the ball away from the younger kid, because I value respect for others."

    > "I feel annoyed when the bell rings and I'm in the middle of solving a math problem because I like to complete what I start."

3. Ask students: *What comes up for you when you hear this?*

4. Ask your class to discuss.

Supporting Activities (for Follow-on Exploration: *Don't Give Others Power Over Your Feelings*)

- Teacher Practice: Notice when you give your power away by using language that suggests that other people are the cause of your feelings. Practice linking your feelings to your needs: I feel _____ because I need _____.

- Listen for times when you (or your students) say: "You make me _____." Ask yourself (or your students) whether you want to give away your power by making someone else responsible for how you feel.

Curricular Tie-ins (for Follow-on Exploration: *Don't Give Others Power Over Your Feelings*)

In your studies of literature:

Look for instances in literature where a character says, "You make me _____."

Try to translate the message into an empowering statement that the character might make: When this happens, I feel _____, because of my need for _____.

POWER 5 ▪ The Power to Observe

TEACHER PREPARATION

Advance Preparation for Modules 5a and 5b

- ☐ Assemble the materials required for each module (see Materials lists on the pages that follow).

- ☐ Photocopy the Notes from the No-Fault Zone narrative script from both modules for two to four student readers.

- ☐ Photocopy the Facts and Message for both modules.

- ☐ Post the Facts and Message for Module 5a at your classroom Message Station at the beginning of the day you will cover Module 5a.

- ☐ Post the Facts and Message for Module 5b at your classroom Message Station at the beginning of the day you will cover Module 5b.

The well-being of Earthlings depends on their ability to observe reality—to see and report just the facts.

Vocabulary for Power 5

(These words are used in Modules 5a and 5b and in following modules. You may want to review these terms with your students before or during the modules.)

- ◉ thoughts
- ◉ misunderstanding
- ◉ negative thoughts
- ◉ stories
- ◉ jumping to conclusions
- ◉ labels
- ◉ trigger

- ◉ observation
- ◉ reality
- ◉ thinking
- ◉ thought habits
- ◉ stories
- ◉ accurately

Module 5a: Observation

Objective: To learn skills for observing reality in order to see accurately what's happening, make wise choices, solve problems, and prevent and resolve conflicts

Activities:

- ☐ Volunteers read Notes from the No-Fault Zone, Facts and Message (15 minutes)

- ☐ Exploration: *What Are Observations?* (15 minutes)
  Type of Activity: Construction, teacher-led discussion

- ☐ Exploration: *Is That an Observation?* (30 minutes)
  Type of Activity: Group decision making

- ☐ Follow-on Exploration: *Make an Observation* (30-minute optional exercise for a different day than the day you do Module 5a)
  Type of Activity: Small-group exercise

Materials:

Materials to prepare in advance:

- ☐ A set of flash cards with one observation or one thought written on each card (from templates in Appendix 2)

- ☐ A box to hold the flash cards

- ☐ 2 8.5" x 11" signs to post on opposite classroom walls: one labeled "**Observation**" and the other, "**Thought**"

Materials for construction:

- ☐ White 3" x 5" index cards (5 per student)

- ☐ Scissors

- ☐ Markers

Materials to be constructed in class during Module 5a:

- ☐ 2 Choice Cards

Materials constructed previously to be used in Module 5a:

- ☐ IOS Power Panels, tokens for Feeling Thermometer, Needs Card Decks, Feelings Card Decks, Energy-Shift Choice Card, photocopied instructions for Energy-Shifting exercises

Materials to be used in the Follow-on Exploration:

- ☐ 100 white 3" x 5" index cards

Get the most accurate information to make choices about life.

Module 5b: Train Yourself to See & Hear Like a Video Camera

Objective: To gain the ability to see and say things clearly by observing what happens as if a video camera were watching and by noticing when thoughts, opinions, stories or interpretations get added to the observations

Activities:

☐ Volunteers read Notes from the No-Fault Zone, Facts and Message (15 minutes)

☐ Exploration: *See Like a Video Camera* (25 minutes)
Type: Video, class discussion

☐ Exploration: *Hear Like a Tape Recorder* (20 minutes)
Type: Audio recording, class discussion

Materials:

Materials to prepare in advance:

☐ Video or DVD player and screen

☐ Video or DVD clip

☐ Tape or CD player

☐ Tape or CD clip of dialogue between two people

☐ Copies of descriptive paragraphs from reading material (only for Supporting Activities)

☑ Materials for Construction: None

☑ Materials to be constructed in class during Module 5b: None

Materials constructed during previous modules to be used again:

☐ Photocopied instructions for Energy-Shifting exercises, Observation and Thought Choice Cards, A set of flash cards with one thought statement written on each card (from templates, constructed for Module 5a)

Module 5a: Observation

Notes from the No-Fault Zone

Michi: Hey! Have you ever wanted to know how scientists think? Why are they able to discover so many new things? That's what we're going to get into today with Power 5: The Power to Observe.

But first, a Power check to make sure you have all your tools. We may not be using them all today but we want you to have them available just in case. Oh yes, you will be receiving two new Choice Cards today to add to your Choice Card Deck. So this is what you should have so far: your IOS Power Panel, Need Cards, Feeling Cards and one Energy-Shift Choice Card. Hold up your Energy-Shift Choice Card when you have all your tools and are ready to go.

[PAUSE until everyone is ready.]

Nao: Okay, let's begin with another look at thoughts. When people have feelings that are too hot or too cold, they often start thinking negative thoughts, telling themselves stories and jumping to conclusions. Then they can't see or hear what is actually happening anymore.

Michi: Do you hear people saying things like, "you're mean," "you're wrong," "you're stupid" or "you're not my friend"?

Nao: I do, so I imagine you do too. These are thoughts in the form of judgments and labels. These thoughts trigger strong feelings in some people.

Michi: And those strong feelings are often the start of arguments and fights.

Nao: Scientists are required to develop their Power to Observe. They look and listen carefully for the facts about what is happening. Then, they write it down. They don't mix in any of their own ideas, anything they have read in a book or heard on TV. They just write down what they see and hear.

Michi: Thoughts can get in the way of observing. Thoughts are like having mud on the windshield of your car: it's hard to see through it.

In the same way, it can be hard to see facts through your thoughts.

Nao: If, in the middle of observing wild gorillas, a scientist starts thinking about what she doesn't like about gorillas or what she thinks they should or shouldn't be doing, she will miss seeing what is in front of her.

Michi: This is an important Power to activate, isn't it?

Nao: It is!

Michi: We're ready to leave on this Exploration. Let's get started developing *your* Power to Observe!

POWER 5a

FACTS

◉ The well-being of Earthlings depends on their ability to observe reality: to see and report just the facts.

◉ Most Earthlings spend a lot of time in their thoughts about reality instead of simply observing reality. When they do this it gets in the way of seeing clearly and often lead to arguments, conflicts and wars.

◉ If they choose, Earthlings can learn to observe reality—and get the most accurate information for making choices about life.

POWER 5a

MESSAGE

Learn to observe reality, like a scientist or detective, and you will increase your ability to do four important things in life:

- See accurately what's happening.

- Make wise choices.

- Solve problems.

- Prevent and resolve conflicts.

Exploration: *What Are Observations?* (15 minutes)

Objective: To recognize the difference between an observation and a thought (or story) about reality

Materials: IOS Power Panels, tokens for Feeling Thermometer, white 3" x 5" index card (1 per student), scissors, pens

Type of Activity: Construction, teacher-led discussion

Procedure:

1. Get to Calm Alert: Ask students to take a Feeling Thermometer read-out. If needed, ask a student to lead an Energy-Shifting exercise so students can get to Calm Alert for this activity.

2. Distribute one white 3" x 5" index card to each student and ask them to make themselves two new Choice Cards: "**Observe Reality**" and "**Add Thoughts to Reality**." (Ask students to cut their index card lengthwise and write one of these two statements on one half, and the other statement on the other half. After this Exploration, ask students to keep these new Choice Cards together with their Energy-Shift Choice Card for future use.)

3. Use or modify this script to introduce the Exploration: *To explore the difference between an observation and a thought, I'd like to read some statements to you. Some are observations of reality and some are thoughts or stories about reality.*

   Here are some observations of reality:

   "I see an apple on the kitchen table."

   "I hear a train whistle."

   "You started talking while I was talking."

   Here are some thoughts added to reality:

   "That apple shouldn't be on the kitchen table."

   "The train is too loud."

   "You're rude."

   Now, I'd like to make some more statements. This time please raise one of your Choice Cards, either "**Observe Reality**" *or* "**Add Thoughts to Reality**," *to indicate the kind of statement you are hearing.*

4. Read the Observation & Thought Statements below one at a time for students to respond to.

Observation & Thought Statements

"You're crazy." (thought)

"He said he didn't agree with you." (observation)

"I'm stupid." (thought)

"I don't understand this problem." (observation)

"You are a thief." (thought)

"You took my pencil when I left my desk." (observation)

"You're mean." (thought)

"You said you'd play with me at recess and you didn't." (observation)

5. Encourage a short class discussion about the difference between observations and thoughts. (If you want, you can ask students to collect observation and thought statements they hear themselves or others say in a journal or on a class list for practice and further discussion.)

Exploration: *Is That an Observation?* (30 minutes)

Objective: To learn to differentiate between observations and thoughts

Materials: Previously prepared flash cards with one observation or one thought statement on each card (see template in Appendix 2), box to hold flash cards, 2 sheets of 8.5" x 11" paper for signs, markers

Type of Activity: Group decision making

Procedure:

1. Make and put up two signs on opposite sides of the room. One sign says "**Observation**," the other sign says "**Thought**."

2. Put the Observation & Thought Statement Flash Cards you have prepared in a box. Ask each student to draw one card from the box.

3. Ask students to read their card silently, then get up and go stand under the sign that they think describes their statement.

4. Ask students under the "**Thought**" sign to read their statements, one at a time.

5. As each student reads their statement, ask students to raise their hand if they agree that the statement is a thought and not an observation. If the class agrees that the statement is actually an observation, the student holding the statement goes to stand under the "**Observation**" sign.

6. Then ask the student who has a flash card that translates the thought into an observation to read their card.

7. As each Thought statement is paired with an Observation statement, the pair of students holding those cards sits down. (If there are still cards remaining in the box after each student has taken one, then some pairs of cards may not be complete. You can ask students to continue drawing from the box until they reach the right Observation match to the current Thought card, or you can wait until all other pairs are formed and then draw from the box until the last students are paired.)

8. Play continues until everyone is sitting down.

9. Ask your class to discuss: *What did you notice? Did you observe anything? Learn anything new?*

10. Ask the dyads now to work together to create new pairs of Observation and Thought cards. Collect the student-made flash cards for future play.

Supporting Activities

- Teacher Practice: Separate your observations of reality from your thoughts and stories about reality, especially when observing your classroom and your students. You can practice by writing down observations of things that occur in class. See what happens.

- Add to your Feelings and Needs Card Decks; ask students to add to their Card Decks.

- Continue to lead or ask students to lead Energy-Shifting exercises, as needed, to practice getting to Calm Alert and to create focus for classroom activities.

- Check in with students about your classroom Group Agreements: Are they working? Are there adjustments or additions anyone wants to suggest to better meet needs in the classroom?

Curricular Tie-ins

In your study of literature:

Read out loud or ask students to read a few passages in literature. Consider using passages that include dialogue between characters, as dialogue gives especially good insight into the concepts in the Power to Observe. Ask students to identify whether the character or the narrator is making an observation or expressing a thought. Ask students to indicate their guesses by holding up one of their new Choice Cards: "**Observe Reality**" or "**Add Thoughts to Reality**."

Follow-on Exploration: *Make an Observation* (30 minutes)

Objective: To learn to translate thoughts into observations

Materials: Set of Thought flash cards used in Module 5a Explorations and/or new Thought flash cards that students make up; extra blank white 3" x 5" index cards (100 cards or 10 cards for each group of 2–4 students); pens or markers

Type of Activity: Small-group exercise

Procedure:

1. Divide students into groups of 2–4.

2. Provide each group of students with 10 Thought flash cards, or ask the groups to make their own cards by writing new statements on blank index card paper, one Thought statement per card.

3. When each group has 10 Thought flash cards in hand, ask the groups to work together to translate each statement into an observation.

4. Ask one person in each group to volunteer to write each group observation statement on a card.

5. When all groups have their 10 Thought statements and 10 translated Observation statements finished, ask each group to share a few with the class.

6. Ask if this Exploration brought up any questions: *Did anyone discover anything new about observations and thoughts during this Exploration?*

7. When this activity has run its course, you can display the pairs of flash cards on the board, and also add these cards to your classroom Observation & Thought flash-card deck for further Explorations.

Most Earthlings spend a lot of time thinking about reality instead of simply observing reality.

Module 5b: Train Yourself to See & Hear Like a Video Camera

Notes from the No-Fault Zone

Nao: Now that you have some experience with recognizing pure observations that have no other thoughts mixed in, you can start listening for them in your everyday activities.

Michi: That can be fun. You might just sit and listen for a few minutes sometime and see how many pure observations you hear and how many observations mixed with thoughts you hear.

Nao: Even though you know something about observations, you might find you don't make them as often as you could. They take some practice, and old habits of mixing thoughts in with your observations can be very strong.

Michi: We are on our way now into another Exploration to help you understand observations better.

POWER 5b

FACTS

⊙ Scientists and detectives train themselves to observe carefully the facts of a situation, as if their eyes and ears were a video camera.

⊙ A video camera records just what it sees, no thoughts, stories, opinions or interpretations added. No one argues with what a video camera records.

⊙ Earthlings can train themselves to see like a scientist or a detective: to observe clearly what is going on.

POWER 5b

MESSAGE

If you want to see and say things clearly, train yourself to observe:

- Train yourself to see like a video camera.

- Notice when you add thoughts, stories or opinions to reality.

Exploration: *See Like a Video Camera* (25 minutes)

Objective: To learn to make visual observations; to practice seeing facts without thinking mixed in

Materials: Video (or DVD) clip and video (or DVD) player, Observation & Thought Choice Cards

Type of Activity: Video, class discussion

Procedure:

1. Introduce the Exploration: *I'd like to review what the Twins said. Why do you think they are recommending that we train ourselves to see like a video camera?*

   To explore how we can learn to see like a video camera, we have two experiments: One is to notice what we see on a video. The other experiment is to notice just what we observe when we take a walk outdoors.

2. Play a short video or DVD clip of people interacting.

3. Give students some instructions for what to watch for: *While watching this short video clip, pretend you are a video camera and notice what happens. I will ask you for your observations afterward.*

4. Stop video after a short scene and ask students what they observed: *I'd like to hear your observations, so I will call on anyone who has an observation to share. If anyone hears any thoughts or story mixed in with the observations, raise your Thought card and I'll call on you to hear what you heard. After each person shares what they saw, if you have something to add, raise your hand.*

Exploration: *Hear Like a Tape Recorder* (20 minutes)

Objective: To learn to make aural observations; to practice hearing facts without thinking mixed in

Materials: Cassette tape or CD clip, tape or CD player, Observation & Thought Choice Cards

Type of Activity: Audio recording, class discussion

Procedure:

1. Play a very short taped dialogue (or a short dialogue from a movie or TV program) for the class.

2. Ask students to volunteer to share what they heard.

3. Ask students who are listening to raise the appropriate Choice Card when they hear either an observation or a thought. If necessary, remind them this is an experiment to train our listening, not a test of who's right or who's wrong.

4. Discuss with students: *What did you notice in this Exploration?*

Supporting Activities

- Teacher Practice: Notice when you express an observation about reality and when you add in thoughts, interpretations or stories.

- Divide the class into pairs, and give each dyad a descriptive paragraph to read. They take turns: One student reads two sentences. The other student says back what was heard. Reflect with students: *What did you notice in this experiment?*

- Experiment: Divide class into pairs. Take a ten-minute walk outside and ask students in pairs to share observations with each other and watch for any thoughts mixed in. When the class is together again, ask what they noticed about making an observation. Ask for volunteers to share any observations of what they saw.

- Add to Feelings and Needs Card Decks.

- Practice Energy-Shifting exercises.

Curricular Tie-ins

In your studies of literature, science, social studies or history:

Notice when characters are adding thoughts or making stories out of the situation or about other people. Notice when characters are making clear observations. Notice what results from these different ways of seeing and different kinds of statements.

POWER 6 ▪ **The Power to Listen**

TEACHER PREPARATION

Advance Preparation for Modules 6a and 6b

☐ Assemble the materials required for each module (see Materials lists on the pages that follow).

☐ Photocopy the Notes from the No-Fault Zone narrative script from both modules for two to four student readers.

☐ Photocopy the Facts and Message for both modules.

☐ Post the Facts and Message for Module 6a at your classroom Message Station at the beginning of the day you will cover Module 6a.

☐ Post the Facts and Message for Module 6b at your classroom Message Station at the beginning of the day you will cover Module 6b.

Vocabulary for Power 6

(These words are used in Modules 6a and 6b and in following modules. You may want to review these terms with your students before or during the modules.)

- ◉ listen
- ◉ listen for feelings and needs
- ◉ communication
- ◉ contribute
- ◉ guess

Module 6a: The 4 Ways to Listen

Objective: To learn about the 4 Ways to Listen and increase students' ability to choose communication that promotes peace and reduces conflict

Activities:

- [ ] Volunteers read Notes from the No-Fault Zone, Facts and Message (15 minutes)

- [ ] Exploration: *The 4 Ways to Listen* (35 minutes)

   Type of Activity: Class exercise

- [ ] Exploration: *Listening Choices* (10 minutes)

   Type of Activity: Construction

Materials:

Materials to prepare in advance:

- [ ] 4 Ways to Listen Chart
- [ ] Blank Feelings List (see Exploration: *Inventory Feelings*)

Materials for construction:

- [ ] White 3" x 5" index cards (2 per student, plus extras)
- [ ] Scissors
- [ ] Pens or markers

Materials to be constructed in class during Module 6a:

- [ ] Feelings List
- [ ] Feelings Card Decks
- [ ] Large Feelings Card Deck for classroom demonstrations

Materials constructed previously to be used in Module 6a:

- [ ] IOS Power Panels, Energy-Shift Choice Card, Need Cards

Materials to be used in the Follow-on Exploration:

- [ ] One deck of Feeling Cards (preferably a large classroom deck that all can see)

No matter if you are sad, scared or excited, it feels good to have someone care enough to stop what they are doing to listen.

Module 6b: Listen for Feelings & Needs

Objective: To practice listening for feelings and needs, recognizing one's own feelings and needs, and guessing at others' feelings and needs

Activities:

☐ Volunteers read Notes from the No-Fault Zone, Facts and Message (15 minutes)

☐ Exploration: *Listen to Each Other* (45 minutes)

Type of Activity: Game

Materials:

✔ Materials to prepare in advance: None

✔ Materials for construction: None

✔ Materials to be constructed in class during Module 6b: None

Materials constructed previously to be used in Module 6b:

☐ IOS Power Panels, Feelings Card Deck, Needs Card Deck

Module 6a: The 4 Ways to Listen

Notes from the No-Fault Zone

Nao: Hi everyone! I'm excited to launch into Power 6: The Power to Listen. But first, let's do our Power check. Make sure you have the following materials ready: Your IOS Power Panel, Need Cards, Feeling Cards and your three Choice Cards. By the way, today you will be adding four more Choice Cards.

[PAUSE until everyone has their materials ready.]

Michi: Power 6 is about learning how to listen. You might be wondering how listening can be a Power since everyone does it. But the truth is that many Earthlings don't know how to listen.

Nao: Many misunderstandings, arguments, fights and even wars are caused because so many (maybe most) Earthlings don't really listen to each other.

Michi: Maybe we could say that everyone hears the words people say, but not everyone listens to find out what the words mean.

Nao: Yes, and that means that when someone learns to listen for the meaning behind words, they have a Power that others don't have. Have you ever had a friend, or your mother or father or teacher, give you their full attention and ask you how you feel and what you need? No matter if you are sad, scared or excited, it feels good to have someone care enough to stop what they are doing to listen.

Michi: And, when we listen for other people's feelings and needs, we have the power to turn enemies into friends.

Nao: That is so true. Listening is way more powerful than most Earthlings realize.

Michi: The following Exploration may reveal some things about listening you haven't thought about before. We hope you find some helpful tips that will boost your Power to Listen.

POWER 6a

FACTS

◉ The well-being of Earthlings depends on their ability to listen for their own feelings and needs, and the feelings and needs of others.

◉ Earthlings talk more than they listen, and when they do listen, they are often busy in their heads listening to their own thoughts instead of listening to one another.

◉ This habit of not really listening causes a lot of misunderstandings, arguments and conflicts.

◉ If they choose, Earthlings can learn to listen for the most important information in their IOS and in the IOS of others: feelings and needs.

POWER 6a

MESSAGE

Learn about the 4 Ways to Listen and you will have more choices in your communication.

The 4 Ways to Listen are:

1. Listen to Thoughts About Me.

2. Listen to Thoughts About You.

3. Listen for My Feelings and Needs.

4. Listen for Your Feelings and Needs.

If you want to connect and understand yourself and other people, reduce conflicts and increase peace, choosing Way 3 and Way 4 works best.

Exploration: *The 4 Ways to Listen* (35 minutes)

Objective: To recognize the four different ways to listen

Materials: 4 Ways to Listen Chart (in Appendix 2, will need to be photo enlarged)

Type of Activity: Class exercise

Procedure:

1. Post the 4 Ways to Listen Chart with its four symbols in a place visible to all in the classroom

2. Review the symbols and hand signals for the 4 Ways to Listen chart with the class.

   (1) Listen to Thoughts About You
   [Index finger pointing out]

   (2) Listen to Thoughts About Me
   [index finger pointing in]

   (3) Listen for Your Feelings and Needs
   [hands in front of chest, facing out]

   (4) Listen for My Feelings and Needs
   [hands in front of chest, facing in]

3. Use the following examples of listening messages to illustrate the 4 Ways to Listen. Say the statement and use the corresponding hand signal:

   ### Listening Examples

   "You talk too fast." [finger pointing out]

   "I'm dumb." [finger pointing in]

   "Are you puzzled and want to know if I've understood you?" [hands at chest outward]

   "I'm confused about the instructions and need clarity." [hands at chest inward]

4. Ask students if they hear the difference between judgments and feelings and needs. Ask if they have any questions about the hand signals.

5. Read through the following listening messages and ask students to use the appropriate hand signals for each statement.

Listening Messages

"You're always bossing me around." [finger pointing out]

"I'm scared and need safety." [hands at chest inward]

"Are you feeling lonely and want company?" [hands at chest outward]

"I'm tired and need rest." [hands at chest inward]

"You never listen to me." [finger pointing out]

"I'm stupid." [finger pointing in]

"Are you feeling proud because you accomplished so much on your project?" [hands at chest outward]

"I'm too loud." [finger pointing in]

"You're mean." [finger pointing out]

"I'm a cry baby." [finger pointing in]

"Are you frustrated and want to understand your math problem?" [hands at chest outward]

"I'm bored and need something interesting to do." [hands at chest inward]

"You talk too much." [finger pointing out]

"I feel angry and need listening." [hands at chest inward]

"I'm lazy." [finger pointing in]

"I feel happy because I got to play." [hands at chest inward]

> Listen for others' feelings and needs, no matter what they say or do.

6. Ask students to notice that the statements with hands at chest outward, Listening for Your Feelings and Needs, are always in the form of a question. This is because nobody can know for sure what other people feel and need. When we make our best guess out loud to someone else, they will usually tell us if we are close or not. The point is not to be right, but to show our interest and care in knowing how they are by listening for their feelings and needs.

Exploration: *Listening Choices* (10 minutes)

Objective: To make four Listening Cards to add to students' Choices Card Decks

Materials: White 3" x 5" index cards (2 per student), scissors, pens or markers

Type of Activity: Construction

Procedure:

1. Hand each student two white 3" x 5" index cards.

2. Ask students to fold each card in half lengthwise so that they can cut on the fold to make two 3" x 2.5" cards.

3. Write on the board the four statements for students to copy, one on each of their new Choice Cards:

   "Listen to Thoughts About Me"

   "Listen to Thoughts About You"

   "Listen for My Feelings and Needs"

   "Listen for Your Feelings and Needs"

Supporting Activities

- Teacher Practice: Notice when you are listening to thoughts and when you are listening for feelings and needs. Notice how you experience the 4 Ways to Listen. Practice listening for feelings and needs, yours and others'.

- During the week, check on students' recognition of the 4 Ways to Listen.

- Continue to add to Feelings and Needs Card Decks.

- Notice opportunities to use the Real-Life Experiment Log, for yourself and for students.

- Check in with students about your classroom Group Agreements. Ask: *Are they working for you?*

Curricular Tie-ins

In your study of literature:

During the week and throughout the year, stop from time to time to ask students: *When you hear the character say what they say, what would you guess their feelings and needs are?*

Ask students to notice in dialogues when characters are listening to thoughts and when they are listening for feelings and needs. Ask students to notice the results of the 4 different Ways to Listen.

Module 6b: Listen for Feelings & Needs

Notes from the No-Fault Zone

Michi: I'm so glad that you have your Feeling Cards and Need Cards now. These tools can make it easier to learn this new language of feelings and needs!

Nao: Some Earthlings say learning feelings and needs is almost like learning a foreign language. It can be uncomfortable at first, and as challenging as learning to speak Russian or Chinese—or learning to speak English for the first time.

Michi: Yes. Tools like the Feeling and Need Cards help a lot, and practice, practice, practice is what it takes to become fluent.

Nao: And there is some listening practice coming up in the next Exploration. We hope you will find it fun and useful in your life.

POWER 6b

FACTS

⊙ When Earthlings listen for their own feelings and needs, they get the essential facts they need to take care of themselves.

⊙ When Earthlings listen for others' feelings and needs, they are able to contribute to others' well-being.

⊙ Earthlings can only make guesses about other Earthlings' feelings and needs. They cannot know for certain if their guess is true until they ask.

POWER 6b

MESSAGE

⊙ Use your Card Decks to help you Listen for Your Feelings and Needs.

⊙ Ask yourself: Right now, what do I feel? What needs are calling for attention?

⊙ Listen for others' feelings and needs, no matter what they say or do. Ask yourself: Right now, what might they feel? What needs are calling for attention?

⊙ Notice whether listening to others' feelings and needs changes the way you see them and understand them.

Exploration: *Listen to Each Other* (45 minutes)

Objective: Practice using listening aids to listen for feelings and needs

Materials: IOS Power Panels, Feelings Card Decks, Needs Card Decks

Type of Activity: Game

Procedure:

1. Ask students to form pairs, or assign them to pairs. In their dyads, ask students to sit next to each other, both facing Player One's IOS Power Panel. Direct all Player Ones to spread their Needs Card Deck out on the desk facing up and to hold their Feelings Card Deck in their hands.

2. Tell the class the first step is for the student who will be Player One to tell their partner about something that happened recently that brought up feelings. Then Player One will lay down a Feeling Card or Cards on the Feelings area of the IOS Power Panel.

3. The second step is for the student who is Player Two to guess a need that Player One might have and ask this question:

   Did you feel _____ (e.g., upset) *because you need or needed* _____ (e.g., understanding, someone to listen to you, kindness)?

4. The third step is for Player One of each pair to say whether the need that was guessed is true for them. If Player One says it is true, Player Two is to place that Need Card on the Needs area of the IOS Power Panel.

5. If Player One disagrees with Player Two's guess, Player One picks up the Need Card that is true for them and places it on the Needs area of the IOS Power Panel. (Remind students that it doesn't matter if the first guess for the need is accurate. Player One will be able to use Player Two's guess to get clear about their needs either way.)

> When we listen for the feelings and needs of others, we have the power to turn enemies into friends.

Example:

Player One: I tried to tell my brother about the game, but he was listening to his music. I felt mad.

[Player One lays down the "**Angry/Mad/Furious/Upset**" Feeling Card.]

Player Two: Did you feel mad because you needed To Be Heard?

[Player One agrees, and Player Two lays down the "**To Be Heard/To Be Understood**" Need Card.]

6. After a Need Card is played, Player One can then say more feelings about the situation or Player Two can ask if there is more to say about it.

7. When one round is complete, ask students to switch roles and for Player Two to use the IOS Power Panel to tell about a situation that brought up feelings. When Player Two lays down a Feeling Card, Player One guesses one or two needs, and so forth.

Variation: *Listening Circle*

The Listening Circle variation of Exploration: *Listen to Each Other* works best with groups of 4–6 students. It provides opportunity for students to be heard and to hear others. Plan on a minimum of 5 minutes per student (20–30 minutes for the entire activity). Ring a bell after each 5 minutes indicating the time to move to the next student. If students have a big situation and need more time for listening, strategize how to give them more time, either during this period or later.

Procedure:

1. Ask students, in groups of 4–6, to sit in a circle on the floor.

2. Direct each group to spread out a deck of Need Cards in the space between them, with the Needs facing up for all to see.

3. Ask a student to begin by holding a deck of Feeling Cards. Player One is to tell a short story of something that happened that brought up feelings, then select and lay down the Feeling Cards for the feelings that came up.

4. Next, ask each student one at a time around the circle to take a turn guessing the need that was connected to the feelings. Ask them to both verbalize their guess ("Were you needing _____?") and also to pick up the corresponding Need Card from the center of the circle and place it in front of Player One (the student who told the story).

5. After each student in the circle has had a turn to guess a need, Player One responds by saying which needs were or are most important in the situation they shared. Player One can also pick up new Need Cards from the center pool.

6. Play continues until each student has had a chance to tell their situation and have classmates guess their needs. Aim for each round to last about 5 minutes.

Supporting Activities

- Teacher Practice: Develop the habit of listening for feelings and needs: your own, your students, your colleague and any characters you notice in your classroom curriculum. This will become more habitual as you practice, and it will bring you a clearer, deeper understanding of yourself and others. When it seems like listening for feelings and needs could contribute to clarity and/or to making connection with students, guess out loud: *Are you feeling _____ because you need _____?*

- Ask for a Full Show of Cards (directions below).

Full Show of Cards

Materials: IOS Power Panels, Feelings Card Decks, Needs Card Decks

Procedure:

1. Ask: *Right now, what are you feeling and what do you need?*
2. Ask students to select Feeling Cards and place them on their IOS Power Panels.
3. Ask students to select Need Cards and place them on their Power Panels.
4. Ask: *Does anyone want to share their feelings and needs?* Students who choose can show their cards or say out loud what they are.
5. If students express Hot or Cold feelings, or if for any reason you sense they could use more listening, ask whether they would like to be listened to more. If students say they would like to have more listening now, and there is time for this, you can ask them to put more Feeling and Need Cards on the Power Panel and share them with class. If they say they would like listening later, you can schedule a time to talk. If at the later time, students have difficulty expressing themselves, they can lay Feeling and Need Cards on their Power Panel for you to read and discuss.

Curricular Tie-ins

In your studies of social studies, history or literature:

During the week and throughout the year, stop from time to time to ask students: *What do you guess this person or character was feeling and needing when they said what you heard them say? Or when they acted in the way that they did?*

POWER 7 ▪ **The Power to Navigate the Fault Zone**

TEACHER PREPARATION

Advance Preparation for Modules 7a and 7b

☐ Assemble the materials required for each module (see Materials lists on the pages that follow).

☐ Photocopy the Notes from the No-Fault Zone narrative script from both modules for two to four student readers.

☐ Photocopy the Facts and Message for both modules.

☐ Post the Facts and Message for Module 7a at your classroom Message Station at the beginning of the day you will cover Module 7a.

☐ Post the Facts and Message for Module 7b at your classroom Message Station at the beginning of the day you will cover Module 7b.

Vocabulary for Power 7

(These words are used in Modules 7a and 7b and in following modules. You may want to review these terms with your students before or during the modules.)

- Fault Zone
- Black & White Thinking
- complain
- blame
- demand

- label
- defuse
- anger
- Anger-Producing Thoughts

Module 7a: The Land of Black & White Thinking

Objective: To increase students' choices by learning to recognize the kinds of thoughts that lead to arguments and conflicts, and learning more conflict resolution and problem-solving tools

Activities:

- ☐ Volunteers read Notes from the No-Fault Zone, Facts and Message (15 minutes)
- ☐ Exploration: *More Choices* (10 minutes)
  Type of Activity: Construction
- ☐ Exploration: *Black & White Thinking* (35 minutes)
  Type of Activity: Small-group discussion, role play
- ☐ Follow-on Exploration: *Get to Know Your Black & White Thinking* (optional exercise: with a 10-minute class introduction and 1-week student journaling exercise) Type of Activity: Self-observation

Materials:

Materials to prepare in advance:

- ☐ 4 sheets chart paper with one of the following headings written on each (see Exploration: *Black & White Thinking*): "**B&W Thinking: COMPLAIN**"; "**B&W Thinking: BLAME**"; "**B&W Thinking: LABEL**"; and "**B&W Thinking: DEMAND**"

- ☐ 4–8 slips of paper with scenarios on them (photocopy the list of scenarios at the end of Exploration: *Black & White Thinking* and cut the pages so each slip shows one scenario, or write your own scenarios if you prefer)

Materials for construction:

- ☐ Chart paper (4 large pieces, prepped per below)
- ☐ Markers
- ☐ White 3" x 5" index cards (2 per student, plus extras)
- ☐ Scissors

Materials to be constructed in class during Module 7a:

- ☐ Choice Cards

Materials constructed previously to be used in Module 7a:

- ☐ IOS Power Panels, large classroom IOS Power Panel, tokens for Feeling Thermometer, Needs Card Decks, Feelings Card Decks, Choices Card Decks

Materials to be used in the Follow-on Exploration:

- ☐ Paper, pencils

Take a closer look at Black & White Thinking.

Module 7b: Crack the Anger Code

Objective: To increase students' power to prevent and resolve conflicts by understanding and learning to D.E.F.U.S.E. anger.

Activities:

☐ Volunteers read Notes from the No-Fault Zone, Facts and Message (15 minutes)

☐ Exploration: *D.E.F.U.S.E. Anger* (45 minutes)

Type of Activity: Teacher-led discussion, construction

☐ Follow-on Exploration: *Translating Shoulds into Needs* (25-minute optional exercise for a different day than the day you do Module 7b)

Type of Activity: Teacher-led discussion

Materials:

✔ Materials to prepare in advance: None

Materials for construction:

☐ White 3" x 5" index cards (1 per student)

☐ Pens or markers

☐ Scissors

Materials to be constructed in class during Module 7b:

☐ New Choice Card: "**D.E.F.U.S.E. My Anger**"

☐ D.E.F.U.S.E. Anger Chart (template in Appendix 2)

Materials constructed previously to be used in Module 7b:

☐ IOS Power Panels, Needs Card Decks, Feelings Card Decks, Choices Card Decks, large classroom IOS Power Panel

✔ Materials to be used in the Follow-on Exploration: None

Module 7a: The Land of Black & White Thinking

Notes from the No-Fault Zone

Nao: Hi everyone! Today we're going to explore another area in your Internal Operating System: the Fault Zone. We hope to shed some light in the dark corners of the Fault Zone so we can see what operates there. Today you will also receive four more Choice Cards. So let's get started with our Power check. Please check to see if you have the following: Your IOS Power Panel, your Need Cards, your Feeling Cards and seven Choice Cards.

[PAUSE until everyone's ready to listen.]

Michi: Okay, here we go into the Fault Zone. Do you ever hear yourself complaining, blaming or calling other people names? Or, maybe you don't say these things out loud but you think them. Do you ever find yourself getting angry with yourself or with other people?

Nao: These are all good signs that you are hanging out in the Fault Zone.

Michi: And, we know that you are not going to have much fun until you find a way out of there.

Nao: In the Power to Navigate the Fault Zone, you will get to take a closer look at Black & White Thinking and Anger.

Michi: So, the Fault Zone is a zone of Inner Space that doesn't have much color to it. There, things are thought of as either good or bad, either right or wrong.

Nao: There are a lot of rules in this zone, and the rules have strict punishments if they are broken.

Michi: It's easy to feel afraid in this zone.

Nao: It is also easy to have very hot or very cold feelings. Some people get angry and some feel sad or depressed when they hang out in this zone for very long.

Michi: Does this sound familiar at all? I suggest you get ready for an interesting adventure! We hope you bring back from this adventure some new understanding about yourself and others.

POWER 7a

FACTS

- The well-being of Earthlings depends on their ability to see when they're in the Fault Zone and to know how to get to the No-Fault Zone.

- Complaining, blaming, labeling and judging are kinds of Black & White Thinking that land Earthlings in the Fault Zone. If this thinking continues, they can stay in the Fault Zone for a long time.

- The longer Earthlings stay in the Fault Zone, the more arguments and conflicts they create and experience.

  - If they choose, Earthlings can learn how to get from the Fault Zone to the No-Fault Zone.

POWER 7a

MESSAGE

⊙ Learn about the Black & White Thinking that takes you to the Fault Zone and keeps you there.

⊙ Find out what choices you have that help you get to the No-Fault Zone when you want to.

Exploration: *More Choices* (10 minutes)

Objective: To add more choices; to add to conflict resolution and problem-solving tools

Materials: White 3" x 5" index cards (2 per student, to make 4 new Choice Cards), scissors, pens or markers

Type of Activity: Construction

Procedure:

1. Hand out two white 3" x 5" index cards to each student.

2. Ask students to cut each card in half to make four 3" x 2.5" cards.

3. Ask students to write one Black & White Thinking Choice word on each card: "**B&W Thinking: Label**," "**B&W Thinking: Complain**," "**B&W Thinking: Blame**" and "**B&W Thinking: Demand**."

It is easy to feel afraid in the Fault Zone.

Exploration: *Black & White Thinking* (35 minutes)

Objective: To introduce the Fault Zone and explore the Black & White Thinking that rules there; to provide options to Black & White Thinking and ways to get to the No-Fault Zone

Materials: IOS Power Panels, tokens for Feeling Thermometer, large class IOS Power Panel (posted on the wall for reference), 4 large pieces of chart paper, markers, slips of paper with scenarios on them (scenarios provided at end of instructions), all the Choice Cards collected from previous modules, 4 new Choice Cards ("**B&W Thinking: Label**," "**B&W Thinking: Complain**," "**B&W Thinking: Blame**" and "**B&W Thinking: Demand**"), Feelings & Needs Card Decks

Type of Activity: Small-group discussion, role play

Procedure:

1. Get to Calm Alert: Ask students to take a Feeling Thermometer read-out. If needed, ask a student to lead an Energy-Shifting exercise so students can get to Calm Alert for this activity.

2. Introduce the Exploration by pointing out the Fault Zone on a large classroom IOS Power Panel so that all can see. Use this script to start with:

    The Twins have asked us to explore this area of our IOS, the Fault Zone. The Fault Zone is ruled by certain kinds of thinking, Black & White

Thinking, and we're going to explore four kinds of Black & White Thinking today. We'll also explore what choices we have when we're in the Fault Zone.

The four kinds of Black & White Thinking are: Label, Complain, Blame and Demand.

3. Ask students to discuss what these four types of thinking are:

   What's an example of Label?

   of Complain?

   of Blame?

   of Demand?

4. Divide the class into 4 groups. Use this script as a guide:

   I'd like us to divide into four groups. Each group will get one of these kinds of Black & White Thinking to Explore, and then you can share with the class what you discovered.

5. Give each group a large piece of chart paper that has one of the following written on it:

   "B&W Thinking: LABEL"

   "B&W Thinking: COMPLAIN"

   "B&W Thinking: BLAME"

   "B&W Thinking: DEMAND"

6. Give each group a slip of paper with a scenario written on it (select one from the list of scenarios on the next page or make up your own).

7. Ask each group to discuss and record on their chart what it would sound and look like if someone responded to the scenario with the type of Black & White Thinking listed at the top of their chart: labeling, complaining, blaming or demanding.

8. Ask students who offer thought statements to be written on their group chart also to describe the reactions that they have to their statement. Others in the group can also contribute their reactions. (Reactions are likely to include feelings and feeling temperature, thoughts, actions, grimaces and body language.)

9. After 15 minutes of discussion and writing, ask each group to take a turn sharing their chart with the group—reading their thought statements and sharing their reactions to the statements.

10. When all four groups have shared their charts, ask the class this question: *So what are your choices when you are in the Fault Zone? Look through your Choice Cards and see what you could choose to do.* (Remind students to look through all their Choice Cards, not just the 4 new ones.)

11. Ask students to volunteer to share one choice they could make when they are in the Fault Zone. After each time a student offers a choice, ask the student this question (they can ask for help from the class if they like): *What do you think would result from that choice?*

Scenarios for Exploration: *Black & White Thinking*

You are feeling so excited to give your report that you are almost jumping out of your seat when your teacher asks who wants to give their report first. Then she calls on someone else.

You're at the animal park with your family and you want to run ahead to see more animals, but your mom says you need to go slower to stay with the family.

You are still in your pajamas and drawing a big picture when your mom comes into your room and says you have to hurry up to get ready for school.

You want to play a game with some kids, but they have already started and say it's too late to join the game.

Your class is putting on a play, and you have read the parts and have been practicing a part that you really want. The director of the play chooses another student for that part, even though that student hasn't looked at the play at all.

Someone throws the ball to you with a lot of force. You can't catch it, and it hits you in the head.

You're standing in line after recess, and another student runs up and gets in front of you.

For the third night in a row, your family has something for dinner that you really don't like.

A friend comes over to your house, and you want to play with just the two of you, but your little brother wants to hang around. When you ask him to go away he doesn't.

All week you and your friends have wanted to play basketball at recess, but every day two groups of older students get to the basketball courts first.

You don't understand the math problems that you are given and you're not sure what questions to ask to get more understanding, so you keep quiet in class and get more and more confused.

You're having so much fun playing with your friend at the park that you don't want to stop when your dad says it's time to go home.

Supporting Activities

- Teacher Practice: Notice what you do when you find yourself in the Fault Zone. Become aware of the choices you have and the results of those choices.

- When it seems students have lost sight of the choices they have for solving a problem or conflict, remind them to look through their Choice Cards and consider the range of choices they have and what might result from the different choices. Students can pair up and help each other do this.

- Continue to introduce and practice Energy-Shifting exercises (see Appendix 3).

- Notice opportunities for you or students to use Real-Life Experiment Logs (template in Appendix 2).

Curricular Tie-ins

In your studies of literature, social studies or history:

Notice when characters are in the Fault Zone and when they are in the No-Fault Zone, and what happens next.

When reading stories or watching videos, note the language of the characters and stop to identify the different kinds of Black & White Thinking and what results the characters achieve from the Black & White Thinking. Pick a scene and ask students, individually, or in pairs, to read through their Choice Cards and choose an action that might have the best results.

Follow-on Exploration: *Get to Know Your Black & White Thinking* (10 minutes in-class time)

Objective: To practice recognizing B&W Thinking; to develop self-awareness; to increase choices

Materials: Paper, pencil

Type of Activity: Self-observation

Procedure:

1. Ask students to keep a diary of their B&W Thinking for one week. Each time they hear themselves label, complain, blame or demand, they record the event in their diary. (See the model below: the exercise is to mark numbers of events, not to write down thought statements or reactions, although students may do that as well if they want to.)

2. Review the types of B&W Thinking before students start their diaries.

   Labeling (good or bad, smart or stupid): You focus on giving people labels rather than finding out what YOU need.

   Complaining (should, ought to, must, have to): You focus on what others should do rather than on what YOU need.

   Blaming (I'm right, you're wrong): You focus on looking for who is to blame rather than finding out what YOU need.

   Demanding (telling others what to do): You focus on commanding rather than making requests.

Get to Know Your Black & White Thinking

For one week keep track of how many times you use shoulds, labels, blame and demands.

Labeling	ℍℍ ℍℍ ‖
Complaining	ℍℍ ‖‖
Blaming	ℍℍ
Demanding	‖‖

Module 7b: Crack the Anger Code

Notes from the No-Fault Zone

Nao: The Fault Zone might be one of the most important parts of your IOS for you to get to know, especially if you are someone who gets angry a lot.

Michi: When Earthlings are angry they often say and do things they don't really mean and then feel bad later.

Nao: Anger is a confusing emotion.

Michi: Yes, and getting to know how anger works gives Earthlings more Power to Navigate the Fault Zone.

Nao: We hope that the Exploration you are going to take now will give you a new understanding of what Anger is and what is hidden behind it.

Michi: You will also receive a new Choice Card: "**D.E.F.U.S.E. My Anger**."

POWER 7b

FACTS

⊙ Anger is a highly charged mixture of feelings and thoughts that often contributes to conflicts.

⊙ Most Earthlings see only two choices when they are angry: to act it out or to sit on it.

⊙ Earthlings can learn a third choice: to crack the Anger Code and find the needs buried inside.

POWER 7b

MESSAGE

⊙ Discover the true cause of anger.

⊙ Learn to D.E.F.U.S.E. Anger so you can get to needs.

Exploration: *D.E.F.U.S.E. Anger* (45 minutes)

Objective: To determine what students already know about detecting and defusing anger; to learn a process for defusing anger; to learn how to get to the root of anger and connect with needs instead

Materials: IOS Power Panels, tokens for Feeling Thermometer, large classroom IOS Power Panel (may be useful to post on the wall for reference), D.E.F.U.S.E. Anger Chart, Card Decks (Feelings, Needs, Choices), white 3" x 5" index cards (1 per student to make 1 "**D.E.F.U.S.E. My Anger**" Choice Card), scissors, pens or markers

Type of Activity: Teacher-led discussion, construction

Procedure:

1. Get to Calm Alert: Ask students to take a Feeling Thermometer read-out. If needed, ask a student to lead an Energy-Shifting exercise so students can get to Calm Alert for this activity.

2. Share this special message from the Twins to introduce the Exploration:

    Two Choices When You Are Angry

    There are two choices available when you have Anger-Producing Thoughts:

    1) You can believe them and feed them. With this choice, you turn your power over to your thoughts. They will steadily grow, because angry thoughts grow more angry thoughts. They can grow uncontrollably into big tangled thought grenades.

    Or

    2) You can D.E.F.U.S.E. them and uncover the hidden message about the needs in your IOS. When you uncover the need behind the anger, you will be able to think more clearly about what action to take to serve your needs best.

3. Write on the board:

    D

    E

    F

    U

    S

    E

4. Discuss what the word *defuse* means. Then, one at a time, add to the board the word from the chart below that corresponds with each letter and explain what it means:

D etect that you are angry.

E ject *should* thoughts.

F ocus on shifting your energy.

U ncover the need behind the anger.

S it with your need.

E xplore possibilities to meet the need.

6 Steps to Crack the Anger Code: D. E. F. U. S. E.

Detect that you are angry. [Hold the Feeling Card for anger]

Notice your signals for anger:

> sweaty palms
>
> red, hot face
>
> narrowed eyes
>
> clenched jaw
>
> tight arm or leg muscles
>
> desire to hurt someone
>
> desire to hurt yourself
>
> other?

Eject *should* thoughts.

Focus on shifting your energy. [Do an Energy Shifter]

Uncover the need behind the anger. [Find the appropriate Need Card]

Sit with your need. [Hold the Need Card in your hand for at least one minute]

Explore possibilities to meet the need.

5. Ask students to make a "**D.E.F.U.S.E. My Anger**" Choice Card to add to their Choices Card Decks. Hand each student one white 3" x 5" index card. Ask students to fold their card in half lengthwise so that they can cut on the fold to make two 3" x 2.5" cards. Then ask them to use one of their new cards to write in "**D.E.F.U.S.E. My Anger**" from the board. (They can save the other, blank card for future modules or to replace older Choice Cards that may be getting worn out.)

6. Ask for volunteers to make a "**Crack the Anger Code: D.E.F.U.S.E.**" poster for the classroom.

Supporting Activities

- Teacher Practice: Use the D.E.F.U.S.E. process when you feel angry. With practice, you will be able to guide students in this process.

- Continue to add to Need Cards and Feeling Cards.

- Notice opportunities to use the Real-Life Experiment Log to learn from mis-takes.

Curricular Tie-ins

In your studies of literature:

1. Select a passage in which a character is angry.

2. Ask students to pretend they are this character who is angry. (Students can get their "Angry" card out of their Feelings Card Deck and hold it.)

3. Explain to students that you are going to conduct an experiment to see what can happen if a character's angry thoughts are fed by continuing to label and blame others.

4. Suggest some sample B&W Thinking phrases that fit the character's situation:

   "He's wrong."   "She's always _____."

   "She should _____."   "He's never _____."

   "He's mean (or bad)."   Other: "_____."

   "She's stupid."

5. Ask students what feelings might get stirred up in the character if she or he keeps saying more and more angry thoughts out loud? (Students can select Feeling Cards and lay them out.)

6. Discuss with the class: *How might the character feel in his or her body? What would you guess is their feeling temperature read-out?*

7. Discuss with the class: *What choices does the character have?*

Follow-on Exploration: *Translating Shoulds into Needs*
(25 minutes)

Objective: To see the need(s) behind the word *should*; to shift angry reactions into needs-based responses

Materials: None

Type of Activity: Teacher-led discussion

Procedure:

1. Share the following information with students: *"Shoulds" are Anger-Producing Thoughts.*

2. Ask students: *Does this statement seem true to you?* Discuss.

3. Share this statement: *If you're thinking somebody should or shouldn't be doing something, you're probably headed for a conflict. You're likely to be getting into somebody else's business, and they won't want to listen to you. I'm curious how you feel when you hear statements like, "You should try harder." Or, "You shouldn't talk like that."* Discuss. (You can collect more examples of *should* statements from students and write them on the board if you like.)

4. Share this example and statement: *Andy takes the ball from you. If you begin thinking "She shouldn't do that," you are starting down the path toward anger. If you think "Somebody should do something about mean students like this," you are taking two more steps down the path of anger—one step for the "should" and another step for the label "mean."*

5. Ask students: *What happens when you think someone should do something? To explore this, think of a time when you thought that someone else should do something. What was your thought? How did you feel when you had that* should *thought?*

6. Discuss student responses. (Angry, upset and frustrated are likely, as well as others.)

7. Explain: *These angry, upset, frustrated feelings produce even more Anger-Producing Thoughts.*

8. Explain: *What I find helpful to remember is that behind every* should *thought, there is a need that is important to me. If you can stop and notice your Anger-Producing Thoughts, and translate them into needs before you believe them and your feeling temperature goes up, you can prevent conflicts.*

9. Ask students: *I'd like to do some detective work to discover the needs behind our* should *thoughts. Does anyone have a* should *thought we can work with?* Discuss.

10. Ask students: *How might you use this information about anger in your daily life at school or at home?*

Supporting Activities

• Teacher Practice: Notice *should* thinking, in yourself and in others. Notice how you feel when you think *should* thoughts. Notice what happens afterward. Uncover the needs behind the *shoulds*.

Curricular Tie-ins

In your study of literature:

Look for hidden should messages in dialogue between characters. Try to guess the need(s) behind the shoulds.

POWER 8 ▪ The Power to Co-operate to Solve Problems & Conflicts

TEACHER PREPARATION

Advance Preparation for Modules 8a and 8b

☐ Assemble the materials required for each module (see Materials lists on the pages that follow).

☐ Photocopy the Notes from the No-Fault Zone narrative script from both modules for two to four student readers.

☐ Photocopy the Facts and Message for both modules.

☐ Post the Facts and Message for Module 8a at your classroom Message Station at the beginning of the day you will cover Module 8a.

☐ Post the Facts and Message for Module 8b at your classroom Message Station at the beginning of the day you will cover Module 8b.

Vocabulary for Power 8

(These words are used in Modules 8a and 8b and in following modules. You may want to review these terms with your students before or during the modules.)

- problem
- conflict
- mission
- puzzle
- prevent
- arguments
- problem solving

- co-operate
- solutions
- win-win solutions
- navigate
- strategy
- charged emotions

Module 8a: Problem Solving

Objective: To learn to co-operate with other people to solve problems and resolve conflicts using the 9 Steps to Solutions

Activities:

☐ Volunteers read Notes from the No-Fault Zone, Facts and Message (15 minutes)

☐ Exploration: *A Problem-Solving Mission—9 Steps to Solutions* (45 minutes)

Type of Activity: Teacher-led discussion, construction, role play

Materials:

Materials to prepare in advance:

☐ 9 Steps to Solutions Chart (template in Appendix 2)

☐ A selected problem between 2 people to describe to the class (you can use a problem between two characters in the literature that you are studying or between two people in your history studies, or one of the problems in the list of scenarios for the Exploration: *Black & White Thinking* in Module 7a)

Problems and conflicts are just puzzles to solve.

Materials for construction:

☐ White 3" x 5" index cards (2 per student)

☐ Light blue 3" x 5" index cards (1 per student)

☐ Scissors

☐ Pens or markers

☐ Pencils

Materials to be constructed in class during Module 8a:

☐ Choice Cards, Observations card

Materials constructed previously to be used in Module 8a:

☐ IOS Power Panels, large classroom IOS Power Panel, Needs Card Decks, Feelings Card Decks, Choices Card Decks

Module 8b: Group Problem Solving

Objective: To learn to co-operate to solve group problems and resolve group conflicts using the 9 Steps to Solutions

Activities:

- ☐ Volunteers read Notes from the No-Fault Zone, Facts and Message (15 minutes)

- ☐ Exploration: *Group Conflict Resolution Mission* (45 minutes)

    Type of Activity: Class exercise

Materials:

Materials to prepare in advance:

- ☐ A real-life group conflict that is going on in your classroom (students may want to help select this)

- ☐ Photocopies of steps 6 and 7 of the procedures for the Exploration (optional: useful if students are to help guide the 9 Steps to Solutions process)

Materials for construction:

- ☐ Chart paper (2 sheets)

- ☐ Easel or blue tape

- ☐ Markers

Materials to be constructed in class during Module 8b:

- ☐ List of observations

- ☐ List of strategies

Materials constructed previously to be used in Module 8b:

- ☐ IOS Power Panels, Needs Card Decks, Feelings Card Decks, Choices Card Decks, 9 Steps to Solutions Chart

Module 8a: *Problem Solving*

Notes from the No-Fault Zone

Nao: Hi everyone! We have been traveling Inner Space together with you for a long time now, and our part of this guided tour is coming near its end. You may not realize it, but you now have many new skills for solving problems and conflicts co-operatively. We are very excited about that!

Michi: And in this Power we are going to take you on two new missions: a Problem-Solving Mission and a Conflict-Solving Mission. You will be asked to gather all your Powers for these missions. So let's do a Power check now and make sure you have: Your IOS Power Panel, Need Cards, Feeling Cards and twelve Choice Cards.

[PAUSE until everyone is ready.]

Nao: First we want to say that problems and conflicts really aren't very different from each other. When you learn the steps for solving a problem, you are well on your way to being able to resolve a conflict.

Michi: And problems are just puzzles to solve. When you know the needs of the people having the problem, you have an important key to unlock the puzzle and solve the problem. Needs are everywhere.

Nao: In the classroom or at home, there are always so many needs going on at once, and there are always many different ideas about how to meet those needs. Is it any wonder that problems come up all the time?

Michi: You all have many Powers now to prevent problems from turning into arguments and fights.

Nao: We know that these skills can be helpful to you in school and at home. In fact, your problem-solving skills will be helpful to you in many ways, wherever you go and whatever you do, for the rest of your lives.

Michi: We hope that this first Problem-Solving Mission reveals many new ways for you to have more fun and act more effectively in your life.

POWER 8a

FACTS

⊙ The well-being of Earthlings depends on their ability to co-operate to solve problems and resolve conflicts.

⊙ If they choose, Earthlings can develop these skills.

⊙ Problems are simply puzzles to solve.

⊙ Earthlings turn problems into conflicts when they don't have skills to identify and meet their own needs.

⊙ Earthlings turn problems into conflicts when they are afraid their needs can't be met.

POWER 8a

MESSAGE

⊙ Learn the 9 Steps to Solutions.

⊙ Use the 9 Steps to Solutions to keep you in the No-Fault Zone.

Exploration: *A Problem-Solving Mission—9 Steps to Solutions* (45 minutes)

Objective: To learn to co-operate with other people to solve a problem and resolve a conflict

Materials: 9 Steps to Solution Chart (template in Appendix 2), white 3" x 5" index cards (1 per student to make 2 new Choice Cards: "**Problem Solve**" and "**Make a Request**"), scissors, pens, light blue index cards (1 per student to make 1 blank Observations card), pencils, a problem between 2 people to use for this exercise (teacher or students can select this), IOS Power Panels, large classroom IOS Power Panel (posted so everyone can see it), Card Decks (Feelings, Needs, Choices)

Type of Activity: Teacher-led discussion, construction, role play

Procedure:

1. Introduce the activity: *Today we get to put together all we have learned so we can solve problems to meet needs for everyone. Every day there are problems to solve, some small and some bigger. Some of these problems turn into conflicts if we take them into the Fault Zone.*

    However, we now have ways to navigate the Fault Zone. We know how to get to the No-Fault Zone where we have all the tools we need to create win-win solutions to problems. With practice we can increase our power to co-operate to solve problems in a way that works for everyone.

    Please gather the following tools for today's Exploration: your IOS Power Panel, Feeling Cards, Need Cards and all your Choice Cards plus 2 new ones: "**Problem Solve**" *and* "**Make a Request**."

2. Hand out 1 white 3" x 5" index card to each student and ask students to make these 2 new Choice Cards by folding the card in half lengthwise, cutting it in half along the fold, and writing one new choice on each: "**Problem Solve**" and "**Make a Request**."

3. When students have their new Choice Cards completed, continue the activity: *You will also need a pencil and a blank Observation card to fill out. Hold on to these for now.* Pass 1 blank light blue index card to each student.

4. Post the 9 Steps to Solution Chart (from Appendix 2) at the front of the class and read through each step together.

5. After reviewing the 9 Steps to Solution Chart, continue: *To practice these steps, we're going to work through a problem together, starting with a problem that involves two people. Everyone will work with a partner for this Exploration.*

6. *Here's the problem we are solving today:* [Describe for your students a problem between two characters in the literature that you are studying, or between two people in your history studies. Another possibility is to select one of the problems in the list of scenarios for the Exploration: *Black & White Thinking* in Module 7a.]

7. Ask for 2 volunteers to come to the front of the room to play the characters in the problem, with both characters starting in the Fault Zone.

8. After the skit, ask the actors to sit down again, then ask all the students these questions:

    What choices did they make in the Fault Zone?

    What were the results?

    What choices could these characters make to begin the Problem-Solving steps? (Hint: Look through your Choice Cards.)

Needs are everywhere.

9. Review the Twins' definition of *conflict*: Conflicts take place in the Fault Zone. People in a conflict are afraid their needs won't or can't be met.

10. Ask students: *What kinds of reaction happen when someone is afraid their needs won't be met?* (Some possibilities: charged emotions, B&W Thinking, a battle in the Fault Zone.)

11. Divide students into pairs, then continue: *Sit across from your partner, with your IOS Power Panels in front of you and touching in the middle. I will be guiding you through the 9 Steps to Solutions that will help you solve this problem.*

12. Taking the 9 Steps to Solutions step by step:

    Step 1. Get to Calm Alert

    If your starting point is in the Fault Zone, take a minute to review your choices and find a way you can get to Calm Alert.

    Step 2. Make an Observation

    Make an observation about the situation: Observe as if you were a video camera.

    Write an observation of the situation on your blue card and place it in the Observations area of your IOS Power Panel.

Step 3. Recognize the Feelings

Lay down a Feeling Card (or several Feeling Cards) to express your feelings about the situation.

Step 4. Recognize the Needs

Lay down a Need Card (or several Need Cards) that identify the need(s) that are calling for attention.

Step 5. Switch Places

Change seats with the other person so you can see into their IOS Power Panel.

Step 6. See from the Other Person's Point of View

Student One, please read from Student Two's IOS Power Panel, out loud, like this: "I see your observation is _____. You're feeling _____, because your needs are _____. Is that right?"

Student Two, please respond: Did Student One guess right? You can add to your observations, feelings and needs at this point if you want.

Then switch parts, so Student Two reads from Student One's IOS Power Panel.

Step 7. Ask the Problem-Solving Question: *How can we meet everyone's needs?*

Look together at the Need Cards in the middle of your IOS Power Panels and think of 3 strategies that could meet both of your needs.

Step 8. Choose a Strategy

Choose one strategy that both of you are willing (with good feelings) to try.

As you consider each strategy, ask yourself: "Am I willing to try this strategy (with good feelings)?" *Choose a strategy only if each person in the situation is willing to try it, without any fear, resentment or sense that they* have *to try it.*

Step 9. Make a Request, Hear a Request

Look at the strategies you have come up with, and each of you make a request of the other.

Your request might sound like this: "I would like to try _____. Would you be willing to try that for three days?"

If you each say yes to the other's request, you have completed the problem-solving circle.

Write down a date to meet again. The time element is important. The idea is to try something and check back in a few days to see how it's working. If it's not working, another strategy can be requested, agreed upon and tried.

If one person says No, *either now or when you meet again, continue to think of more possible strategies until both parties in the situation can say* Yes.

14. Ask if any students want to share something about their experience with the group.

15. Hold a discussion with the whole group: *Do you see ways these problem-solving steps could work with real-life problems between you and someone else?*

Supporting Activities

• Teacher Practice: Practice the 9 Steps to Solutions when you have a problem to work out within yourself or with someone else.

• Support students in using the 9 Steps to Solutions to solve their own problems and conflicts. If the other person involved in a student's problem is a classmate and is willing, they can both bring their IOS Power Panel and Card Decks to the table. If the other person involved in the problem is not a classmate, a student can ask a classmate to play the part of the other person and play their cards on their IOS Power Panel as if they are that person.

• Continue to practice Energy-Shifting exercises. This can be especially helpful when there is a problem or conflict.

• Check in with students about your classroom Group Agreements: *How are our Group Agreements working? Do they support meeting needs in the classroom?*

• Notice opportunities for students to fill out Real-Life Experiment Logs, to learn from mis-takes.

Curricular Tie-ins

In your studies of social studies, history, current events or literature:

When you notice that two people in your curriculum materials have a problem to solve, divide up the parts and ask two students to demonstrate for the class how the problem could be solved, using their IOS Power Panels and Card Decks. Or divide students into pairs and have each pair work with the same problem.

Module 8b: *Group Problem Solving*

Notes from the No-Fault Zone

Nao: Today we would like you to use your problem-solving skills to solve a group conflict. Different people can choose to play different parts. Your teacher will explain the parts to you in a few minutes.

First, let's do a Power check: Make sure you have the following tools ready: Your IOS Power Panel, Need Cards, Feeling Cards and fourteen Choice Cards.

[PAUSE until everyone has their materials and is ready to listen.]

Michi: To go on this Conflict-Solving Mission, we would like you to use a real conflict that is going on between groups of students. Feelings for some of you might get hot or cold. That is part of working with conflict.

Nao: If every member of the group plays his or her part, we are sure that you can find a strategy to solve the conflict that everyone is willing to try.

Michi: Yes, and if it doesn't work, we know, and we hope you know, that you and your classmates have the skills to keep looking for new strategies until you find one that does work.

Nao: We have heard reports that sometimes people feel confused or puzzled for a while when they are in the middle of this mission. This one can be a bumpy ride.

Michi: We also have heard that things get clearer as you go. So, if you are willing and ready, please put on your seat belts and let's get this mission started.

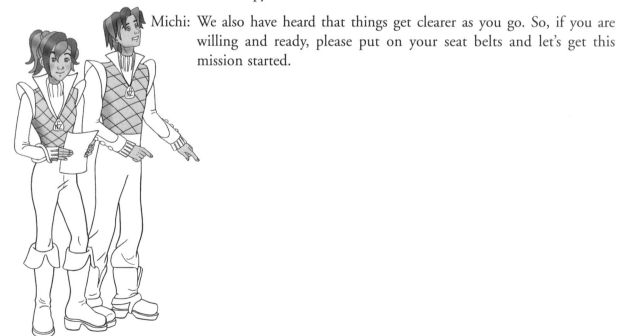

POWER 8b

FACTS

- Group problems are puzzles to solve.

- Earthlings can learn to co-operate in groups to solve problems with care for everyone's needs.

POWER 8b

MESSAGE

⊙ Use the 9 Steps to Solutions to solve group problems.

⊙ Learn as a group how to create a No-Fault Zone in your classroom.

Exploration: *Group Conflict Resolution Mission* (45 minutes)

Objective: To learn to co-operate to solve problems and resolve conflicts in groups

Materials: 9 Steps to Solutions Chart, a real-life group conflict that is going on in your classroom (students may want to help select this), IOS Power Panels, Card Decks (Feelings, Needs, Choices), Problem-Solve Choice Card (*How can we meet everyone's needs?*), blank chart paper, easel or blue tape, markers, photocopies of steps 6 and 7 of the Procedures below (optional: useful if students are to help guide the 9 Steps to Solutions process)

Type of Activity: Class exercise

Procedure:

1. Post the 9 Steps to Solutions Chart in a place where everyone can see it.

2. Introduce the Exploration: *The Twins have asked us to apply what we've learned so far about resolving problems to a conflict we have in our classroom (or our school). The same 9 Steps to Solutions that we used to problem solve between two people can also be used to resolve a group conflict. Today we will work on a real-life conflict we have in the class.*

3. Select and describe a conflict that involves a group of students (it doesn't have to directly involve all the students), or ask students to help you select a conflict to use for this Exploration.

4. Ask students to volunteer to be Problem Solvers, Recorders or Active Observers (if they are not involved in the conflict or if for any reason they would prefer to participate by observing).

5. Ask students to sit in a circle on the floor with their IOS Power Panels, Feelings and Needs Card Decks, and Choices Card Deck. Ask Problem Solvers to place their IOS Power Panels in front of them. Ask each Active Observer to sit near and observe a Problem Solver or to use their own Power Panel and Card Decks to follow along and observe the group process.

5. Guide students through the 9 Steps to Solutions. Optional: You can ask if any students acting as Recorders would like to help guide the process by taking turns reading one problem-solving step at a time and giving students time to do the step. (You will need blank chart paper and markers available to make lists once you start the process. Make copies of steps 6 and 7 below for volunteer Recorders to read if you choose to have students guide the process.)

> You can prevent problems from turning into arguments or fights.

6. Start Where You Are: Ask students involved in the group process, *Where are you in Inner Space? Are you in the No-Fault Zone or are you in the Fault Zone? Look into your IOS: Take a Feeling Thermometer read-out. Notice if you have any Black & White Thinking.*

7. Use the suggested scripts below to follow the 9 Steps to Solutions.

Get to Calm Alert (Step 1)

If you are not able to get to Calm Alert on your own, ask someone in the class to help you by listening to your feelings and needs or doing an Energy-Shifting exercise with you.

(It may be helpful for the whole class to begin with an Energy-Shifting exercise if feelings about this conflict are charged.)

Make an Observation (Step 2)

When everyone is at Calm Alert, ask Problem Solvers to raise their hands to make an observation about the situation. When everyone agrees that a student has made an observation (rather than a complaint), they can place their "**Observe Reality**" Choice Cards on their Power Panels. Other students can add to the observation one at a time. Write each of the observations that come up on chart paper on the wall, or ask a student Recorder to do so. Continue until students are satisfied that what is written on the chart paper describes the situation.

If students have difficulty making clear observations, you can ask, *Is that a view a video camera would see? Does anyone hear a judgment or label? If so, can you suggest an observation?*

Recognize the Feelings (Step 3) &

Recognize the Needs (Step 4)

Ask all Problem Solvers to sort through and place Feeling Cards and Need Cards that represent their feelings and needs in the situation out on their IOS Power Panels. Remind students that if they want help, they can ask a classmate who is an Active Observer to help them sort out their feelings and needs.

Ask Recorders to circulate through the class and put together a classroom Power Panel with all the Feeling and Need Cards that the Problem Solvers have come up with.

When each student Problem Solver finishes placing all their own Feeling and Need Cards on their Power Panel, they also can volunteer to help a classmate who hasn't completed these steps.

When all students have placed their cards on their Power Panels, ask: *Are there any Problem Solvers who would like to share their feelings and needs with the group?*

Switch Places (Step 5) &

See from the Other Person's Point of View (Step 6)

When all relevant Feeling and Need Cards are on the Power Panels in the center and have been shared verbally by those who wish to do so, ask students to get up and walk around the outside of the circle and read and notice all the needs that their classmates are asking to be addressed. (A Recorder may want to make a list of these for when the classroom Power Panel read-out is dismantled at the end of the Exploration.)

Ask the Problem-Solving Question (Step 7) & Choose a Strategy (Step 8)

Then ask students to go back to their own IOS Power Panel and sit down. Ask if any will volunteer suggestions for solutions that could meet all the needs. Write suggestions on the board or a new page of chart paper, or ask a student Recorder to volunteer to do this. Repeat this goal as often as needed: *Our goal is to decide together on a strategy: one solution that everyone is willing to try.*

Crack the Anger Code and find the needs buried inside.

Make a Request, Hear a Request (Step 9)

When it seems that a strategy has been agreed upon, ask a few students to volunteer as representatives from each side of the issue to make requests from the other side's representatives. Ask them to use this template: "We would like to try _____. Would you be willing to try that for one week?"

When each side agrees to the other's request, you have completed the group conflict resolution circle. Mark a day to meet again on the classroom calendar.

The time element is important. The idea is to try something and check back in a few days to see how it's working. If it's not working, discuss what it is that's not working. Students may think of an adjustment to the strategy and want to try again. Or they may agree to try a different strategy either from your list or from the new discussion.

8. Lead a group discussion. Ask Problem Solvers about their experience: *How was it to follow the 9 Steps to Solutions in a group?* Ask Active Observers and Recorders to share what they observed. Share your own observations of the process.

Supporting Activities

- Teacher Practice: Spend some time reflecting on the Group Problem-Solving process you experienced. What worked well? What would you do differently next time? You may want to fill out a Real-Life Experiment Log to get more clarity, so you can set up the process in a way that students can benefit from throughout the year.

- Support students in using the 9 Steps to Solutions process when they have a group conflict or problem.

Curricular Tie-ins

In your study of history or current events:

When studying conflicts between groups in history, students can take sides in the conflict and use the 9 Steps to Solutions process to resolve the conflict together. For example, if studying the Civil War, half the students could represent the South and half the North. Or, if studying Native Americans and the European colonists to America, half the students could represent the Native Americans and half could represent the colonists.

POWER 9 ▪ The Power to Create a No-Fault Zone Wherever You Are

TEACHER PREPARATION

Advance Preparation for Modules 9a and 9b

☐ Assemble the materials required for each module (see Materials lists on the pages that follow).

☐ Photocopy the Notes from the No-Fault Zone narrative script from both modules for two to four student readers.

☐ Photocopy the Facts and Message for both modules.

☐ Post the Facts and Message for Module 9a at your classroom Message Station at the beginning of the day you will cover Module 9a.

☐ Post the Facts and Message for Module 9b at your classroom Message Station at the beginning of the day you will cover Module 9b.

Vocabulary for Power 9

(These words are used in Modules 9a and 9b. You may want to review these terms with your students before or during the modules.)

- ⊚ ever-widening
- ⊚ circles
- ⊚ connection
- ⊚ Circles of Connection
- ⊚ ripples
- ⊚ pebble
- ⊚ activated
- ⊚ co-create
- ⊚ community
- ⊚ envision
- ⊚ gradually

Earthlings have the power to create what they can envision and are willing to work for.

Module 9a: Inner Circles of Connection

Objective: To review what students have learned about preventing and resolving conflict with themselves and others since beginning the *No-Fault Classroom* curriculum; to add to the Classroom Vision and Group Agreements; to meet needs for completion and closure

Activities:

☐ Volunteers read Notes from the No-Fault Zone, Facts and Message (15 minutes)

☐ Exploration: *What Do You Know?* (10 minutes)

Type of Activity: Teacher-led discussion

☐ Exploration: *Re-envision, Re-agree* (35 minutes)

Type of Activity: Class discussion, review

Materials:

☑ Materials to prepare in advance: None

Materials for construction:

☐ Chart paper

☐ Easel or blue tape

☐ Markers

Materials to be constructed in class during Module 9a:

☐ Circles of Connection Chart

☐ Additions to Classroom Vision and Group Agreements

Materials constructed previously to be used in Module 9a:

☐ Vision drawings and poems made during the first Class Meeting

☐ Group Agreements made in the second Class Meeting

Module 9b: Outer Circles of Connection

Objective: To envision a community, city, nation, world/planet that students would like to live in; to envision ways students can contribute to that world; to meet needs for closure and celebration

Activities:

☐ Volunteers read Notes from the No-Fault Zone, Facts and Message (15 minutes)

☐ Exploration: *The Outer Circles of Connection* (45 minutes)

Type of Activity: Small-group project

Materials:

☑ Materials to prepare in advance: None

Materials for construction:

☐ Markers

Materials to be constructed in class during Module 9b:

☐ Circles of Connection Chart (additions)

Materials constructed previously to be used in Module 9b:

☐ Circles of Connection Chart

When you work
with others, your
Powers are
greater.

Module 9a: Inner Circles of Connection

Notes from the No-Fault Zone

Nao: Everyone's lives are made up of ever-widening Circles of Connection, starting with ourselves and our family and then moving out to include our neighborhood and the friends and acquaintances we have there. As you grow older, your circle will move out even more to include your school—teachers, whole classrooms of people your own age, and students who are older and younger than you are. Bigger schools and more friends are yet to come, and then your Circles of Connection will widen even beyond that.

Michi: Let's stop there. We don't want to get too far ahead of ourselves. Would someone volunteer to draw on the board three circles inside one another—like the ripples that form when you throw a pebble in a pond.

[PAUSE to select a volunteer and for the volunteer to draw these circles.]

Nao: The center circle represents you. The second circle represents you moving out to interact with friends in your neighborhood, and the third circle represents you moving into a larger circle of interaction—your classroom.

Michi: And, inside of each of you is a No-Fault Zone. Not everyone knows about the No-Fault Zone or how to get to it. In many people, their No-Fault Zone hasn't been activated yet.

Nao: You are different. As you have been constructing your No-Fault Classroom, step-by-step and Exploration-by-Exploration, you have been activating the No-Fault Zone inside of you.

Michi: Now, whenever you have a problem or whenever you're in a conflict, it is your choice to go to the Fault Zone or to go to the No-Fault Zone to try to solve it.

Nao: The mission Michi and I came here to carry out is almost finished. We now have just three more Explorations to take before we say our good-bye.

Michi: Today we'll go on two Explorations. We will look back on where we have been together and then look forward to what you want for your classroom between now and the end of the school year.

Since I know you all are experienced explorers of Inner Space, I would like to get started on these Explorations right away. Would that be alright with you, Nao?

Nao: Sure! Let's go!!

POWER 9a

FACTS

⦿ The well-being of Earthlings depends upon their ability to go to the No-Fault Zone when they have a problem to solve or a conflict to resolve.

⦿ If they choose, Earthlings can develop the ability to co-create No-Fault classrooms, schools and communities.

⦿ If they choose, Earthlings can develop the ability to co-create a world where everyone's needs matter.

⦿ Earthlings have the power to create what they can envision and are willing to work for.

⦿ Earthling's Powers are greater when they work with others than when they work alone.

POWER 9a

MESSAGE

⊙ Create a vision for what you want. Share your vision with others.

⊙ Work together to create the classroom you want.

⊙ Start envisioning the world you want to live in and developing the skills you need to create it.

Exploration: *What Do You Know?* (10 minutes)

Objective: To create awareness of Circles of Connection; to review what has been learned about how to connect with self, others and the classroom to solve problems and conflict; to meet needs for completion and closure

Materials: Chart paper, easel or blue tape, markers

Type of Activity: Teacher-led discussion

Procedure:

1. Introduce the activity: *The Twins have introduced us to the three inner Circles of Connection.*

2. *The innermost circle is connecting with ourselves.* Label the top of a piece of chart paper "**Circles of Connection**" and post it on the wall. Draw a small circle on the chart and label it "**Self.**"

   What information do you have about yourself now that you didn't have when we started the No-Fault Classroom? What information do you have now that contributes to problem solving and conflict prevention and resolution within yourself?

   Listen to student responses. (Possibilities: How to identify feelings and needs, observe reality without thoughts mixed in, get from the Fault Zone to the No-Fault Zone, Get to Calm Alert, D.E.F.U.S.E. My Anger.)

3. *The second Circle of Connection, as we move outward, is connecting with another person.* Draw a second circle outside the first and label it "**Other.**"

   What information do you have about connecting with others that you didn't have when we started the No-Fault Classroom? What information do you have now that contributes to problem solving and conflict prevention or resolution between you and another person? (Possibilities: How to identify another person's feelings and needs, not take personally the things others say and do, Problem Solve, give others time and support to get out of the Fault Zone before interacting.)

4. *The third Circle of Connection is connecting with your classroom.* Draw the third circle outside the others and label it "**Classroom.**" *What information do you have about connecting with a classroom that you didn't have when we started the No-Fault Classroom? What information do you have now that contributes to problem solving and conflict prevention or resolution in the classroom?* (Possibilities: How to use Power Panels and Card Decks to problem solve with a group.)

Keep your Powers activated by using them as much as you can.

Exploration: *Re-Envision, Re-Agree* (35 minutes)

Objective: To add to the Classroom Vision; to add to the Group Agreements; to meet needs for completion and closure

Materials: Vision drawings and poems students made during the first Class Meeting (or photograph of group collages), Group Agreements made in the second Class Meeting (and revised along the way), chart paper, easel or blue tape, markers

Type of Activity: Class discussion, review

Procedure:

A. Classroom Vision Statement

1. Introduce the discussion: *At the beginning of our No-Fault Classroom construction project, we talked about a Vision for the classroom. I have the drawings and poems all of you made at that time.* Hand out drawings and poems to the students who created them.

2. *I'd like to review our Classroom Vision with you. What did we set out to create?* Write these responses on the board or on chart paper on the wall. Add your responses as well.

3. *How successful have we been at doing what we set out to do?* Listen to responses. Share your own responses.

4. *Based on what we have been learning, can you think of anything else you would like to add to our Vision?* Make a list on a piece of chart paper of new suggestions to add to the Classroom Vision. Students later may create new artwork or poems to add to the classroom collage.

B. Group Agreements

1. Introduce the discussion: *As you know, at the beginning of our No-Fault Classroom project, we made Group Agreements to ensure safety, trust and as much learning as possible. We have looked at it and added to it since we created it. I'd like to review that Agreement with you at this point. Has it created safety and trust and learning for ALL of you?*

2. *Based on what we have been learning, can you think of anything else you would like to add to our Agreements?* (If all students agree to a suggestion, add the suggestion to the Group Agreements.)

3. You could suggest adding an agreement like the following to the Group Agreements and seeing if all students will agree: "Use our IOS Power Panels and Card Decks of Feelings, Needs and Choices for problem solving and conflict resolution for a month." (Note that the

Start envisioning the world you want to live in.

time element is important so the class can review and revise agreements. We hope that an agreement like this one will serve to create peace for everyone for the remainder of the year.)

Curricular Tie-ins

In your studies of literature, history or science:

Look at situations in the lives of characters in literature or figures in history and science and determine what Circles of Connection they were experiencing at the time. For example, Helen Keller, when she learned to communicate through signs, was connecting with her family. Later, when she learned to speak and read and write, she connected with the world of her time (1880–1968).

Module 9b: Outer Circles of Connection

Notes from the No-Fault Zone

Michi: This is a time to look to the future and to celebrate!

Nao: Yes, it is. Thinking about the future, it might seem hard to believe, but you will be finished with elementary school, middle school and high school before you know it.

Michi: There are a lot of steps along the way, and every year of your life you will be expanding your Circles of Connection and influence.

Nao: Gradually you will have more opportunities and choices in the Outer Circles of Connection.

Michi: Along with the fun and excitement that you have ahead, you might have some bumpy times when challenges and fears seem like road-blocks. But you now have your Powers activated, and you will always have them with you wherever you go, no matter what you do.

Nao: Daily problems aren't going to go away. Over and over again, you will have the chance to choose to check in with your IOS and go to the No-Fault Zone or not. It will always be your choice.

Michi: We hope that as you go traveling more and more in your Outer Circles of Connection, you will remember your travels to Inner Space with us.

Nao: And, we hope that you will keep your Powers activated by using them as much as you can.

Michi: The No-Fault Zone inside you never disappears, but it's possible to forget how to get to it if you choose not to use your Powers.

We hope that you will remember us, and when you do, you'll remember the way back to the No Fault-Zone.

Nao & Michi: Good-bye for now. You will always be on our radar. Please come visit our home in the No Fault-Zone, any time you choose.

POWER 9b

FACTS

◉ There are Outer Circles of Connection beyond the classroom. These include your school community, your city, your country and the world.

◉ You have the power to help form and influence these Outer Circles.

◉ One way you do this is by knowing about your Internal Operating System and carrying within you a No-Fault Zone. This will enable you to create a No-Fault Zone wherever you are and wherever you go within your Circles of Connection.

POWER 9b

MESSAGE

⊙ You can start now to envision the world you want to live in. You can start now to work with others to create it.

⊙ Continue to steer by your IOS, which gives you True-to-You Power.

⊙ See how to create a No-Fault Zone wherever you go.

⊙ Increase the Peace.

Exploration: *The Outer Circles of Connection* (45 minutes)

Objective: To increase awareness of Outer Circles of Connection; to participate in a group process to envision a community, city, nation and world/planet that students would like to live in; to envision how students can contribute to that world; to meet needs for closure and celebration

Materials: Circles of Connection Chart, markers

Type of Activity: Small-group project

Procedure:

1. Introduce the activity: *The Twins have introduced us to the Outer Circles of Connection, and today I would like to look at them with you to see what we can learn about our influence there.*

2. *The fourth, fifth, sixth and seventh circles are community, city, nation and world/planet.* Draw these circles around the three inner circles on the Circles of Connection Chart and label them "**Community**," "**City**," "**Nation**" and "**World**."

3. Begin a discussion: *Do you think that what we are learning can affect these Outer Circles of Connection to solve problems and prevent, reduce and resolve conflicts? How?*

   The No-Fault Zone inside you never disappears.

4. Create a Classroom Vision for the Outer Circles: *Without a Vision for what we want, it is difficult to make it happen. What kind of community, city, nation and world would you like to help create, and how would you want to contribute to it?*

   Ask students to share their visions for the Outer Circles of Connection: The World We Want to Live In. Then ask them to divide into affinity groups (groups that seem to share a similar vision) to talk about how they want to express their vision and how they might want to contribute to it becoming reality. Below is a beginning list of options for how student visions might be expressed.

   Option 1. **Create a mural:** a large shared image combined with words, phrases, short poems, and pictures and words cut from magazines.

   Option 2. **Create a quilt:** a wall hanging (paper or cloth) made up of each student's 8" x 8" (or whatever size you choose) drawing or poem or collage.

   Option 3. **Write a song or poem:** a work that students can deliver to the class. Copies can be made so all students can sing or recite together. A recording can be made to share with parents or other classrooms.

Option 4. **Other:** Students can determine their own type of contribution to express their vision.

5. Ask students to share their visions with one another as a celebration of the Powers they are developing to contribute to everyone's well-being, and as a way to expand their influence in their world.

Supporting Activities

- Ask students to make a list of the gifts or talents they have and would like to share, then start sharing them with one another.

- Ask students to select an Outer Circle of Connection project that would help meet people's needs for food, water, health, housing, understanding, respect, peace, etc. This could be an individual project or a project for pairs, small groups or the whole class. Research Web sites of projects, research about the need and what others are doing to meet the same need.

- For ideas about contributing to the Outer Circles of Connection, research Web sites (www.myhero.com, www.Giraffe.org, www.kidsface.org) to see how young people are currently contributing to the world they would like to live in.

- For inspiration and encouragement, read biographies about people who have contributed to the Outer Circles of Connections throughout history.

Curricular Tie-ins

In your studies of literature, history or science:

Look at situations in the lives of characters in literature or figures in history and science and determine what Circles of Connection they were experiencing at the time. For example, Galileo, when he shared his research about the Earth circling around the sun, was connecting with the world of his time (1564–1642).

Appendix 1

Observation Survey

Data Collection

If you would like to participate in a data collection experiment about the effects of this program on student interactions, co-operation and participation, we suggest you use the following Observation Survey to (a) establish a baseline, and (b) collect data at four-to six-week intervals.

We expect you will find value in conducting this survey for your own evaluation and learning. If, additionally, you would like to participate in our data collection project, we would greatly appreciate your sending your final data (baseline and progress checks) to contact@k-hcommunication.com. We will publish the results of this data collection on our Web site.

Instructions

Establish a Baseline

Choose three to five times during the week prior to starting the program to observe students during a twenty-minute period of "free time" in the classroom. It is important that this be an active, social time together: playing games, talking, etc. Students are likely to be most relaxed and interactive if the observer is unobtrusive.

- Use the Observation Survey form.

- Check "Baseline" at the top of the form. Fill in the date and length of the observation when you finish.

- Observable Behaviors: Use one tally mark each time you observe one of the listed behaviors during the observation period. It's easy to count up tallies in groups of five—four vertical tallies crossed by a diagonal.

- Additional Information: Complete this section as accurately as possible.

- Notes: Add notes that help describe what you saw.

> Put away the book, the description, the tradition, the authority and take the journey of self-discovery.
>
> —J. Krishnamurti

Check Progress

Every four weeks, or at an interval of your choice, repeat the observation process. Keep the conditions the same: a twenty-minute period of "free time" in the classroom to talk, play games, read, etc.

- Use the Observation Survey form.

- Check "Progress Check" at the top of the form. Fill in the date and length of the observation when you finish.

- Observable Behaviors: Use one tally mark each time you observe one of the listed behaviors during the observation period. It's easy to count up tallies in groups of five—four vertical tallies crossed by a diagonal.

- Additional Information: Complete this section as accurately as possible.

- Notes: Add notes that help you describe what you saw.

Observation Survey _____ Baseline _____ Progress Check

Date _____ Length of Observation _____

Noting length of observation is important if you want to compare data with others or between surveys.

Date school started (baseline) or date of last survey
(progress check) _____

Observable Behaviors

How many times do you:

_____ hear bickering, arguing, blaming

_____ hear put downs, negative judgments

_____ hear complaining

_____ hear demands, commands

_____ hear students saying *should* or *have to*

_____ see aggressive behaviors, fights

_____ remind student(s) about behavior

_____ hear sharing of feelings and needs

_____ hear requests

_____ see students work out their own problems/conflicts peacefully

Additional Information

If establishing a baseline, fill in numbers for the period of time since the beginning of the year. If checking progress, fill in numbers for the period of time since the last survey.

How many students from your class have been:

_____ absent?

_____ tardy?

_____ sent out of the classroom because of their behavior?

_____ sent to detention?

_____ suspended?

Percentage of students who are generally on task with learning: _____

Percentage of time students are focused and productive: _____

Noteworthy changes since the last survey: _____

_____

_____

_____

_____

_____

_____

_____

Notes: _____

_____

_____

_____

_____

_____

_____

_____

_____

_____

_____

_____

_____

_____

Appendix 2

Materials Templates

Contents

- **Internal Operating System** (IOS) Power Panel Template (Introduction to the No-Fault Zone)

- **Charts**

   The 9 Powers (Introduction to the No-Fault Zone)

   4 Ways to Listen (Module 6a)

   6 Steps to D.E.F.U.S.E. Anger (Module 7b)

   9 Steps to Solutions (Module 8a)

- **Card Decks**

   14 Choice Cards (Module 1b)

   14 Need Cards (Module 2a)

   14 Feeling Cards (Module 4a)

- **Worksheets**

   Note of Appreciation (Class Meeting 2)

   Real-Life Experiment Log (Module 3b)

   The Feelings & Needs Connection (Module 4a)

   Feelings vs Thoughts (Module 4b)

   Observation & Thought Statement Flash Cards (Module 5a)

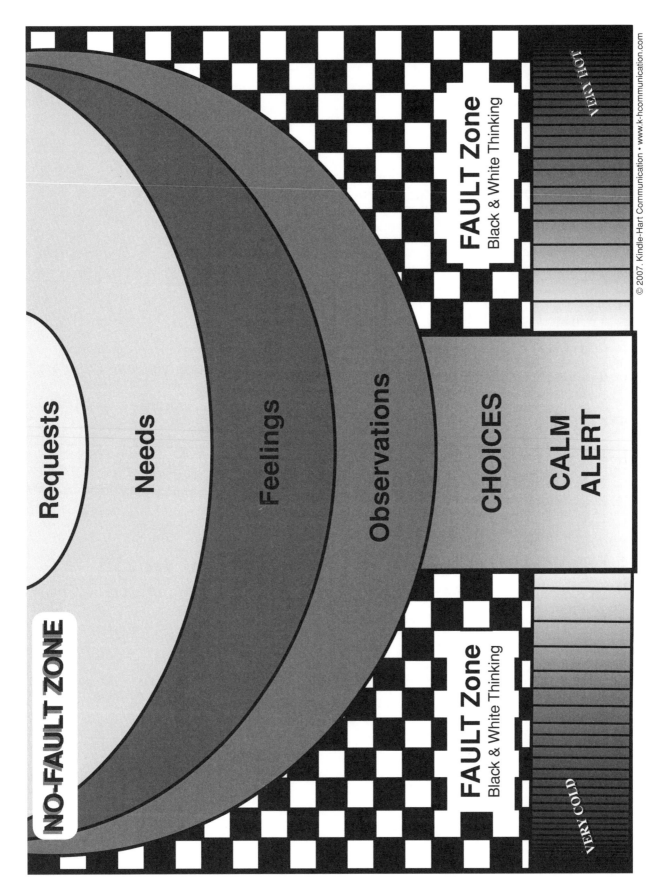

The 9 Powers

1. The Power to Get to Calm Alert

2. The Power to Know What You Need

3. The Power to Find Ways to Meet Needs

4. The Power to Read Feelings

5. The Power to Observe

6. The Power to Listen

7. The Power to Navigate the Fault Zone

8. The Power to Co-operate to Solve Problems & Conflicts

9. The Power to Create a No-Fault Zone Wherever You Are

4 Ways to Listen

1. **Listen to Thoughts About You**
   [index finger pointing out]

2. **Listen to Thoughts About Me**
   [index finger pointing in]

3. **Listen for Your Feelings & Needs**
   [hands in front of chest, facing out]

4. **Listen for My Feelings & Needs**
   [hands in front of chest, facing in]

6 Steps to D. E. F. U. S. E. Anger

Detect that you are angry. [Hold the Feeling Card for anger]

Eject *should* thoughts.

Focus on shifting your energy. [Do an Energy Shifter]

Uncover the need behind the anger. [Find the appropriate Need Card]

Sit with your need. [Hold the Need Card in your hand for at least one minute]

Explore possibilities to meet the need.

9 Steps to Solutions

1. Get to Calm Alert

2. Make an Observation

3. Recognize the Feelings

4. Recognize the Needs

5. Switch Places

6. See from the Other Person's Point of View

7. Ask the Problem-Solving Question:
   How can we meet everyone's needs?

8. Choose a Strategy

9. Make a Request, Hear a Request

Try Out Your Solution and See How it Works

Choice Cards (Module 1b)

Problem Solve How can we meet everyone's needs?	**Make a Request**
Add Thoughts to Reality	**Observe Reality** I see . . . I hear . . . I remember . . .
B&W Thinking **Complain**	B&W Thinking **Blame**
B&W Thinking **Label**	B&W Thinking **Demand**
Listen to **Thoughts About ME**	Listen to **Thoughts About YOU**
Listen for **MY** **Feelings & Needs**	Listen for **YOUR** **Feelings & Needs**
ENERGY SHIFT Get to *Calm Alert*	**D.E.F.U.S.E.** My Anger

Need Cards (Module 2a) • Front Copy

Community   Friends
Belonging

Play • Fun

Rest   Relaxation

To Be Heard
To Be Understood

Need Cards (Module 2a) • Back Copy

Need Cards (Module 2a) • Front Copy

Understanding Others
Empathy

Understanding Me
Self-Empathy

Capability • Competence
Skills

Learning • Exploration
Discovery

Need Cards (Module 2a) • Back Copy

Need Cards (Module 2a) • Front Copy

Choice • Autonomy Freedom

Self-Expression • Creativity

Safety • Trust

Giving • Sharing

Need Cards (Module 2a) • Back Copy

Need Cards (Module 2a) • Front Copy

Help • Support

Respect • To Matter
To Be Considered

Make your own card here

Make your own card here

Need Cards (Module 2a) • Back Copy

Feeling Cards (Module 4a) • Front Copy

Happy • Glad
Delighted   Cheerful

Sad   Unhappy
Disappointed   Lonely

Angry   Mad
Furious   Upset

Curious   Interested

Feeling Cards (Module 4a) • Back Copy

Feeling Cards (Module 4a) • Front Copy

Thankful • Grateful

Playful • Exuberant

Unsettled • Concerned
Tense

Peaceful • Content
Satisfied • Calm • Relaxed

Feeling Cards (Module 4a) • Back Copy

Feeling Cards (Module 4a) • Front Copy

Scared • Worried
Afraid

Excited • Enthusiastic
Energetic • Eager

Confused • Puzzled
Mixed Up • Unsure

Surprised • Shocked

Feeling Cards (Module 4a) • Back Copy

Feeling Cards (Module 4a) • Front Copy

Friendly • Loving
Tender • Warm

Frustrated

Make your own card here

Make your own card here

Feeling Cards (Module 4a) • Back Copy

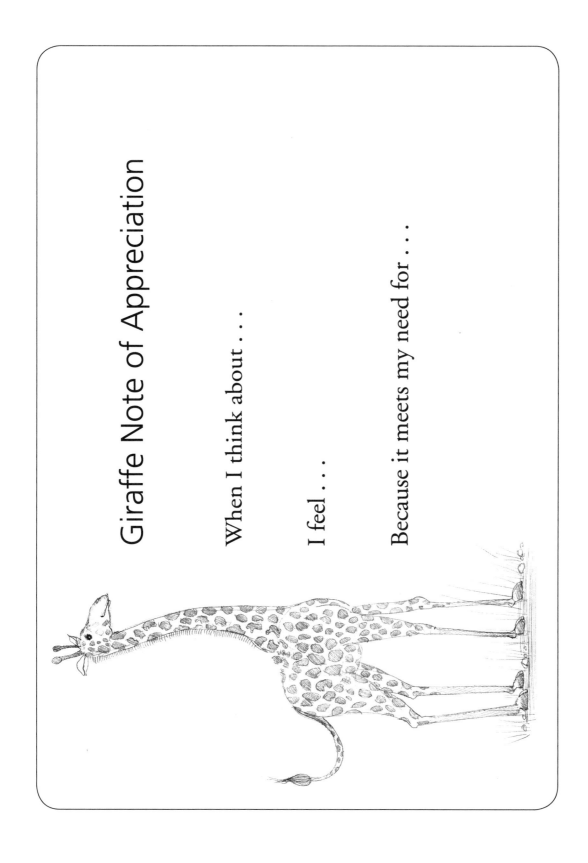

Real-Life Experiment Log

1. What did I do?

_____

_____

_____

2. What was the result?

_____

_____

_____

3. What needs were met?

_____

_____

_____

4. What needs weren't met?

_____

_____

_____

5. What would I do differently next time?

_____

_____

_____

The Feelings & Needs Connection

Think of a time you felt **HAPPY**.

What happened? _____

What NEED was MET? _____

⊙ ⊙

Think of a time you felt **SAD**.

What happened? _____

What NEED was NOT MET? _____

⊙ ⊙

Think of a time you felt **SCARED**.

What happened? _____

What NEED was NOT MET? _____

⊙ ⊙

Think of a time you felt **EXCITED**.

What happened? _____

What NEED was MET? _____

Feelings vs Thoughts Worksheet

Put an (F) next to statements that you believe are feelings and put a (T) next to statements you believe are thoughts.

___ I feel confused.

___ I feel that you didn't explain it very well.

___ I feel scared.

___ I feel frustrated.

___ I feel that you're a smart person.

___ I feel she doesn't like me.

___ I feel hopeful.

___ I'm nervous.

___ I feel it's unfair.

___ I feel safe.

___ I feel you don't understand me.

___ I feel that you do understand me.

___ I feel you should apologize.

___ I feel itchy.

___ I felt left out.

___ I feel dissed.

___ I feel awful.

___ I feel that you are mean.

___ I feel abandoned.

___ I feel unorganized.

Observation & Thought Statement Flash Cards

When you came around the corner and bumped into me, I fell.	**You play too rough.**
I spent two hours doing homework.	**My teacher is mean.**
There's glue on the table and on the floor.	**You always make a mess.**
She told me I had to use blue paint, not green.	**Our teacher is so bossy.**
He kept asking me questions when I was trying to write.	**He is always bugging me.**
I saw you kick the ball onto the roof, then I heard you say you didn't do it.	**You're a liar.**
I hear you talking when I am trying to read.	**You are so annoying.**
I saw you pick up my pencil and put it on your desk.	**You stole my pencil!**

Observation & Thought Statement Flash Cards *(Continued)*

They said no one else could be in their club.	They think they are so cool.
She walked away when we said we didn't want to play kickball.	She's weird.
You didn't move out of my way when I asked you to.	You're stupid. It's your fault that you got hurt.
You told the teacher that I took your pencil.	You're a tattletale.
I ended up bleeding the last time we played together.	You play too rough.
They are pressing their noses against the window.	They're acting stupid.
She burped.	She is so rude.
You are sitting with your legs stretched out.	You look silly sitting like that.

Observation & Thought Statement Flash Cards *(Continued)*

She put mustard on her apple.	She does the weirdest things.
He read two books this week.	He is a slow reader.
You sat on my glasses. Now they are cracked.	You are so clumsy and stupid.
You bumped into me.	You are taking up too much room.
He pushed me out of line.	That's rude.
You stayed inside after I asked you to come out.	You're a stupid idiot.
You ate the last two pieces of pie.	You're a pig.
She said I couldn't join the game.	That's rude.

Appendix 3

Energy-Shifting Exercises

Contents

- Energy-Shifting Exercise Log
- Body Scan
- Heart Breathing
- The Hook-Up
- Tekubi Furi (hand shaking)
- Cross Crawl
- The Neurovascular Hold
- The Tree
- 6-Second Pause
- Self-Empathy

Energy-Shifting Exercise Log

Date _____

Name of Exercise _____

Before the Exercise: Take a Body Scan.

Note sensations, feelings, thoughts.

_____

_____

_____

_____

_____

After the Exercise: Take a Body Scan.

Note sensations, feelings, thoughts.

_____

_____

_____

_____

_____

Body Scan

We get signals from our Internal Operating System about how things are going in our Inner Space: we get feelings of happiness and satisfaction as well as feelings of stress, anger and sadness. When we notice our feelings, we have more choice about how we feel and what we do.

1. Sit on your chair with both feet on the floor and your hands on your knees.

2. Close your eyes. Take a few deep breaths.

3. Bring your attention to your head and neck. Move your head up and down, side to side, and in circles. Feel the heaviness of it. Let it hang forward and relax.

4. Put your attention on your shoulders. Lift them up and down, move them front and back and in circles. Wiggle them.
    Relax them.

5. Lift your arms. Wiggle them and shake them out. Rest them at your side or with your hands on your knees.

6. Shake your hands out. Wiggle your fingers and relax them.

7. Stretch your legs in front of you. Tighten them and relax them two or three times. Shake them.

8. Make circles with your feet, one direction then the other. Place your feet on the floor.

9. Wiggle your toes. Point them and relax them. Place your feet on the floor again.

10. Stop to listen to your body. What word comes up to describe the general feeling of your body? Light? Heavy? Notice your head and neck, shoulders, arms, fingers and hands, legs and ankles, feet and toes.

11. Take five or six deep breaths and then open your eyes.

Energy Shifter: *Heart Breathing**

Use this exercise as a fallback when an energy shift is needed and/or as a way to start the morning.

1. Think of something you are grateful for, something that makes you smile. It could be a pet, a person, a tree or flower.

2. Sit comfortably, close your eyes and relax.

3. Take five slow breaths.

4. Place your hands on the center of your chest.

5. Think of the person, pet or plant that makes you smile. Breathe in the smiling, grateful energy. Breathe this feeling into the area under your hands.

6. Take five more slow breaths.

* *Heart Breathing* is a variation of a HeartMath exercise (www.heartmath.org). The HeartMath system was created by Doc Childre, a stress researcher, author and consultant to leaders in business, science and medicine. HeartMath offers an innovative view of psychology, physiology and human potential that provides a new model for efficient living in the modern world. HeartMath is taught in schools, corporations, government agencies and health care institutions to give people the ability to meet life challenges with resiliency, intelligence and compassion.

⊙ ⊙ ⊙ ⊙ ⊙ ⊙ ⊙ ⊙ ⊙ ⊙ ⊙ ⊙ ⊙ ⊙ ⊙ ⊙ ⊙ ⊙ ⊙ ⊙

Energy Shifter: *The Hook-Up**

This simple routine increases coordination and stabilizes the entire energy system.

1. Stand straight and relaxed.

2. Place the middle finger of one hand on a spot between the eyebrows and just above the bridge of the nose.

3. Place the middle finger of the other hand over the navel.

4. Gently press each finger into the skin, pull it upward and hold for 12–30 seconds.

5. Take a Body Scan and notice the sensations.

* *The Hook-Up* comes from Energy Medicine, developed by Donna Eden. Energy Medicine is based on centuries-old information about the energy meridians of the body and teaches people of all ages to optimize the energy flows in their bodies for optimum health, mental functions and overall well-being.

Energy Shifter: *Tekubi Furi* (hand shaking)*

1. Stand with your feet side by side, about shoulder-width apart, with your weight mostly on the balls of your feet. Keep knees slightly bent and relaxed.

2. With arms at your sides, let your hands shake very quickly. Let the motion cause your heels to bounce slightly up and down. Continue for about 20 seconds.

3. Stop shaking and just stand there and notice the sensation for a moment. Take a Body Scan: What do you notice?

* *Tekubi Furi* is an exercise from Aikido, which is a nonviolent martial art founded by Morihei Ueshiba (1883–1963.) Aikido is a mind-body practice that deals with conflict in a calm, non-aggressive way. Young people and adults take up the practice of Aikido to develop inner balance, strength, flexibility and freedom of movement. In the words of Morihei Ueshiba: "Aikido is not a technique to fight with, nor to defeat the enemy. It is a way to reconcile the world and make human beings one family."

Energy Shifter: *Cross Crawl* *

1. Stand straight with weight distributed equally on both legs.

2. Lift your right arm and your left leg at the same time.

3. As you let them down, raise your left arm and right leg.

4. Repeat this sequence, and exaggerate the lift of your leg and the swing of your arm across the midline of your body.

5. Continue in this exaggerated march, as slowly and smoothly as you can. While you do this, breathe deeply in through your nose and out through your mouth.

* *Cross Crawl* comes from Brain Gym (also called Educational Kinesiology) which was developed by Paul Dennison, PhD, over a period of 25 years. Brain Gym is the study and application of natural movement experiences to facilitate learning and activate the brain for optimal storage and retrieval of information. Brain Gym exercises function to re-educate the mind/body system for accomplishing any skill or function with greater ease and efficiency.

Energy Shifter: *The Neurovascular Hold**

When you feel stress, anger or fear, up to 80 percent of the blood can leave the thinking center of your brain (the frontal lobes). Your thinking may become fuzzy, and you won't be able to think through a situation and stay connected to your needs.

The Neurovascular Hold brings the blood back to the frontal lobes of the brain so you can think more clearly, re-connect with your feelings and needs, and get to Calm Alert.

1. Sit straight and breathe gently and deeply.

2. Place the palm of one hand on your forehead and the palm of your other hand at the back of your head.

3. Feel the energy in your hands bring warmth to your head.

4. Hold softly for up to 3 minutes, breathing gently and deeply.

* *The Neurovascular Hold* comes from Energy Medicine, developed by Donna Eden. Energy Medicine is based on centuries-old information about the energy meridians of the body and teaches people of all ages to optimize the energy flows in their bodies for optimum health, mental functions and overall well-being.

Energy Shifting: *The Tree**

1. Place the palms of your hands together. Place them in the middle of your chest.

2. Lift one knee in front of you so your foot is a few inches off the floor.

3. Hold, breathe and silently count to 20.

4. Repeat on the other side.

5. Make the count longer each time you do this exercise.

To improve balance, look at a spot on the floor a few feet in front of you.

* *The Tree* is a yoga exercise.

Energy Shifter: *6-Second Pause*

Use this exercise to engage your thinking brain (the cortex); to cool down hot sensations of aggravation, irritation or distress; or to wake up the brain when sensations are cold.

Try the following:

1. Count to 6 in a foreign language.

2. Name 6 pets you have known.

3. Feel 6 breaths of air filing your lungs and imagine what it looks like.

4. Remember the names of 6 of the Seven Dwarfs.

Energy Shifter: *Self-Empathy*

1. Sit on the floor or at a table or desk with your Feeling Cards and Need Cards.

2. Close your eyes and take 3–5 deep breaths.

3. Ask yourself, *What am I feeling right now?*

4. Open your eyes, sort through the Feeling Cards and pick out the card (or cards) that match your feelings. Put the card (or cards) on the floor or desk in front of you.

5. Then sort through the Need Cards and put down the Need Cards that match your IOS.

6. Notice how you feel when you know what you need and know how you feel.

Bibliography

Bickmore, Kathy. "Teaching Conflict and Conflict Resolution in School: (Extra-) Curricular Considerations." In *How Children Understand War and Peace: A Call for International Peace Education*, edited by Amiram Raviv, Louis Oppenheimer, and Daniel Bar-Tal, 233–59. San Francisco: Jossey-Bass, 1999.

Childre, Doc Lew and Howard Martin with Donna Beech. *The HeartMath Solution: The Institute of HeartMath's Revolutionary Program for Engaging the Power of the Heart's Intelligence*. New York: HarperCollins Publishers, 2000. First published 1999 by The Institute of HeartMath.

Eisler, Riane. *Tomorrow's Children: A Blueprint for Partnership Education for the 21st Century*. Boulder, CO: Westview Press, 2000.

Eisler, Riane and Ron Miller, eds. *Educating for a Culture of Peace*. Portsmouth, NH: Heinemann, 2004.

Fritz, Robert. *The Path of Least Resistance: Learning to Become the Creative Force in Your Own Life*. New York: Fawcett Columbine, 1989.

Gatto, John Taylor. *A Different Kind of Teacher: Solving the Crisis of American Schooling*. Berkeley Hills Books, 2001.

Glasser, William. *The Quality School: Managing Students Without Coercion*, rev. ed. New York: HarperPerennial, 1998.

Goleman, Daniel. *Emotional Intelligence*. New York: Bantam Books, 1995.

Hart, Sura and Victoria Kindle Hodson. *The Compassionate Classroom: Relationship Based Teaching and Learning*. Encinitas, CA: PuddleDancer Press, 2005. First published 2004 by Center for Nonviolent Communication.

———. *Respectful Parents, Respectful Kids: 7 Keys to Turn Family Conflict into Co-operation*. Encinitas, CA: PuddleDancer Press, 2006.

Hodson, Victoria Kindle and Mariaemma Willis. *Discover Your Child's Learning Style*. Roseville, CA: Prima Publishing, 1999.

Holt, John. *How Children Fail*, rev. ed. Reading, MA: Addison-Wesley Pub. Co., 1982. First published 1964 by Pitman.

———. *How Children Learn*, rev. ed. Reading, MA: Addison-Wesley Pub. Co., 1983. First published 1967 by Pitman.

———. *Learning All the Time*. Reading, MA: Perseus Books, 1989.

Kohn, Alfie. *Beyond Discipline: From Compliance to Community*, 2nd ed. Alexandria, VA: Association for Supervision and Curriculum Development, 2006.

———. *No Contest: The Case Against Competition*, rev. ed. Boston: Houghton Mifflin Co., 1992.

————. *Punished by Rewards: The Trouble with Gold Stars, Incentive Plans, A's, Praise, and Other Bribes*. Boston: Houghton Mifflin Co., 1993.

Kreisberg, Seth. *Transforming Power: Domination, Empowerment, and Education*. State University of New York Press, 1992.

Krishnamurti, J. *Education and the Significance of Life*. San Francisco: Harper & Row, 1953.

Miller, Ron, ed. *Creating Learning Communities: Models, Resources, and New Ways of Thinking About Teaching and Learning*. Brandon, VT: The Foundation for Educational Renewal, Inc., 2000.

Montessori, Maria. *The Absorbent Mind*. New York: Henry Holt & Company, LLC, 1995. First published 1967 by Holt, Rinehart and Winston.

————. *The Secret of Childhood*. Translated by M. Joseph Costelloe. Notre Dame, IN: Fides Publishers, 1966.

Noddings, Nel. *The Challenge to Care in Schools: An Alternative Approach to Education*, 2nd ed. New York: Teachers College Press, 2005.

Palmer, Parker. *The Courage to Teach: Exploring the Inner Landscape of a Teacher's Life*, 10th anniversary ed. San Franciso: Jossey-Bass, 2007.

Pearce, Joseph Chilton. *The Biology of Transcendence: A Blueprint of the Human Spirit*. Rochester, VT: Parker Street Press, 2002.

————. *Evolution's End: Claiming the Potential of Our Intelligence*. HarperSanFrancisco, 1992.

Rosenberg, Marshall. *Life-Enriching Education: Nonviolent Communication Helps Schools Improve Performance, Reduce Conflict, and Enhance Relationships*. Encinitas, CA: PuddleDancer Press, 2003.

————. *Nonviolent Communication: A Language of Life*, 2nd ed. Encinitas, CA: PuddleDancer Press, 2003.

Sahtouris, Elisabet. *Earthdance: Living Systems in Evolution*. iUniverse, 2000.

Schore, Allan N. *Affect Regulation and the Origin of the Self: The Neurobiology of Emotional Development*. Hillsdale, NJ: Lawrence Erlbaum Associates, 1994.

Siegel, Daniel J. *The Developing Mind: How Relationships and the Brain Interact to Shape Who We Are*. New York: Guilford Press, 1999.

Index

How You Can Use the NVC Process

Clearly expressing how **I am** without blaming or criticizing	Empathically receiving how **you are** without hearing blame or criticism

OBSERVATIONS

1. What I observe *(see, hear, remember, imagine, free from my evaluations)* that does or does not contribute to my well-being: *"When I (see, hear) . . . "*	1. What you observe *(see, hear, remember, imagine, free from your evaluations)* that does or does not contribute to your well-being: *"When you see/hear . . . "* *(Sometimes unspoken when offering empathy)*

FEELINGS

2. How I feel *(emotion or sensation rather than thought)* in relation to what I observe: *"I feel . . . "*	2. How you feel *(emotion or sensation rather than thought)* in relation to what you observe: *"You feel . . ."*

NEEDS

3. What I need or value *(rather than a preference, or a specific action)* that causes my feelings: *" . . . because I need/value . . . "*	3. What you need or value *(rather than a preference, or a specific action)* that causes your feelings: *" . . . because you need/value . . ."*

Clearly requesting that which would enrich **my** life without demanding	Empathically receiving that which would enrich **your** life without hearing any demand

REQUESTS

4. The concrete actions I would like taken: *"Would you be willing to . . . ?"*	4. The concrete actions you would like taken: *"Would you like . . . ?"* *(Sometimes unspoken when offering empathy)*

Some Basic Feelings We All Have

Feelings when needs are fulfilled

- Amazed
- Comfortable
- Confident
- Eager
- Energetic
- Fulfilled
- Glad
- Hopeful
- Inspired
- Intrigued
- Joyous
- Moved
- Optimistic
- Proud
- Relieved
- Stimulated
- Surprised
- Thankful
- Touched
- Trustful

Feelings when needs are not fulfilled

- Angry
- Annoyed
- Concerned
- Confused
- Disappointed
- Discouraged
- Distressed
- Embarrassed
- Frustrated
- Helpless
- Hopeless
- Impatient
- Irritated
- Lonely
- Nervous
- Overwhelmed
- Puzzled
- Reluctant
- Sad
- Uncomfortable

Some Basic Needs We All Have

Autonomy
- Choosing dreams/goals/values
- Choosing plans for fulfilling one's dreams, goals, values

Celebration
- Celebrating the creation of life and dreams fulfilled
- Celebrating losses: loved ones, dreams, etc. (mourning)

Integrity
- Authenticity • Creativity
- Meaning • Self-worth

Interdependence
- Acceptance • Appreciation
- Closeness • Community
- Consideration
- Contribution to the enrichment of life
- Emotional Safety • Empathy

Physical Nurturance
- Air • Food
- Movement, exercise
- Protection from life-threatening forms of life: viruses, bacteria, insects, predatory animals
- Rest • Sexual expression
- Shelter • Touch • Water

Play
- Fun • Laughter

Spiritual Communion
- Beauty • Harmony
- Inspiration • Order • Peace

- Honesty (the empowering honesty that enables us to learn from our limitations)
- Love • Reassurance
- Respect • Support
- Trust • Understanding

About PuddleDancer Press

PuddleDancer Press (PDP) is the premier publisher of Nonviolent Communication™-related works. Its mission is to provide high-quality materials that help people create a world in which all needs are met compassionately. PDP is the unofficial marketing arm of the international Center for Nonviolent Communication. Publishing revenues are used to develop and implement NVC promotion, educational materials, and media campaigns. By working in partnership with CNVC and NVC trainers, teams, and local supporters, PDP has created a comprehensive, cost-effective promotion effort that has helped bring NVC to thousands more people each year.

Since 2003, PDP has donated over 50,000 NVC books to organizations, decision-makers, and individuals in need around the world. This program is supported in part by donations to CNVC and by partnerships with like-minded organizations around the world. To ensure the continuation of this program, please make a tax-deductible donation to CNVC earmarked to the Book Giveaway Campaign, at www.CNVC.org/donation

Visit the PDP website at www.NonviolentCommunication.com to find the following resources:

- **Shop NVC**—Continue your learning. Purchase our NVC titles online safely and conveniently. Find multiple-copy and package discounts, learn more about our authors, and read dozens of book endorsements from renowned leaders, educators, relationship experts, and more.

- **NVC Quick Connect e-Newsletter**—Sign up today to receive our monthly e-Newsletter, filled with expert articles, resources, related news, and exclusive specials on NVC learning materials. Archived e-Newsletters are also available.

- **Help Share NVC**—Access hundreds of valuable tools, resources, and adaptable documents to help you share NVC, form a local NVC community, coordinate NVC workshops and trainings, and promote the life-enriching benefits of NVC training to organizations and communities in your area.

- **Pressroom**—Journalists and producers can access author bios and photos, recently published articles in the media, video clips, and other valuable information.

- **About NVC**—Learn more about these life-changing communication skills including an overview of the four-part process, Key Facts about NVC, benefits of the NVC process, and access to our NVC e-Newsletter and Article Archives.

For more information, please contact PuddleDancer Press at:

P.O. Box 231129 • Encinitas CA 92024
Phone: 858-759-6963 • Fax: 858-759-6967
Email: email@puddledancer.com • www.NonviolentCommunication.com

About CNVC and NVC

About CNVC

Founded in 1984 by Dr. Marshall B. Rosenberg, the Center for Nonviolent Communication (CNVC) is an international nonprofit peacemaking organization whose vision is a world where everyone's needs are met peacefully. CNVC is devoted to supporting the spread of Nonviolent Communication (NVC) around the world.

NVC is now being taught around the globe in communities, schools, prisons, mediation centers, churches, businesses, professional conferences, and more. Dr. Rosenberg spends more than 250 days each year teaching NVC in some of the most impoverished, war-torn states of the world. More than 200 certified trainers and hundreds more teach NVC to approximately 250,000 people each year in thirty-five countries.

CNVC believes that NVC training is a crucial step to continue building a compassionate, peaceful society. Your tax-deductible donation will help CNVC continue to provide training in some of the most impoverished, violent corners of the world. It will also support the development and continuation of organized projects aimed at bringing NVC training to high-need geographic regions and populations.

CNVC provides many valuable resources to support the continued growth of NVC worldwide. To make a tax-deductible donation or to learn more about the resources available, visit their website at www.CNVC.org.

For more information, please contact CNVC at:

 5600 San Francisco Rd. NE Suite A, Albuquerque, NM 87109
Ph: 505-244-4041 • Fax: 505-247-0414
Email: cnvc@CNVC.org • Website: www.CNVC.org

About NVC

From the bedroom to the boardroom, from the classroom to the war zone, Nonviolent Communication (NVC) is changing lives every day. NVC provides an easy-to-grasp, effective method to get to the root of violence and pain peacefully. By examining the unmet needs behind what we do and say, NVC helps reduce hostility, heal pain, and strengthen professional and personal relationships.

NVC helps us reach beneath the surface and discover what is alive and vital within us, and how all of our actions are based on human needs that we are seeking to meet. We learn to develop a vocabulary of feelings and needs that helps us more clearly express what is going on in us at any given moment. When we understand and acknowledge our needs, we develop a shared foundation for much more satisfying relationships. Join the thousands of people worldwide who have improved their relationships and their lives with this simple yet revolutionary process.

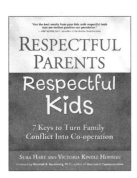

Respectful Parents, Respectful Kids

7 Keys to Turn Family Conflict Into Co-operation

by Sura Hart and Victoria Kindle Hodson

$15.95 — Trade Paper 7.5x9.25, 256pp, ISBN: 978-1-892005-22-9

Stop the Struggle—Find the Co-operation and Mutual Respect You Want!

Do more than simply correct bad behavior—finally unlock your parenting potential. Use this handbook to move beyond typical discipline techniques and begin creating an environment based on mutual respect, emotional safety, and positive, open communication. **Respectful Parents, Respectful Kids** offers **7 Simple Keys** to discover the mutual respect and nurturing relationships you've been looking for.

Use these 7 Keys to:

- Set firm limits without using demands or coercion
- Achieve mutual respect without being submissive
- Successfully prevent, reduce, and resolve conflicts

- Empower your kids to open up, co-operate, and realize their full potential
- Make your home a **No-Fault Zone** where trust thrives

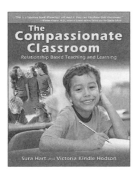

The Compassionate Classroom

Relationship Based Teaching and Learning

by Sura Hart and Victoria Kindle Hodson

$17.95 — Trade Paper 7.5x9.25, 208pp, ISBN: 978-1-892005-06-9

Students Can Resolve Their Own Conflicts!

When compassion thrives, so does learning—Learn powerful skills to create an emotionally safe learning environment where academic excellence thrives. Build trust, reduce conflict, improve cooperation, and maximize the potential of each student as you create relationship-centered classrooms. This how-to guide offers customizable exercises, activities, charts, and cutouts that make it easy for educators to create lesson plans for a day, a week, or an entire school year. An exceptional resource for educators, homeschool parents, child care providers, and mentors.

"Education is not simply about teachers covering a curriculum; it is a dance of relationships. *The Compassionate Classroom* presents both the case for teaching compassionately and a wide range of practical tools to maximize student potential."

—Tim Seldin, president, The Montessori Foundation

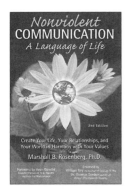

Nonviolent Communication: A Language of Life, Second Edition

Create Your Life, Your Relationships, and Your World in Harmony with Your Values

Marshall B. Rosenberg, Ph.D.

$17.95 — Trade Paper 6x9, 240pp, ISBN: 978-1-892005-03-8

In this internationally acclaimed text, Marshall Rosenberg offers insightful stories, anecdotes, practical exercises and role-plays that will literally change your approach to communication for the better. Nonviolent Communication partners practical skills with a powerful consciousness to help us get what we want peacefully.

Discover how the language you use can strengthen your relationships, build trust, prevent or resolve conflicts peacefully, and heal pain. Over 400,000 copies of this landmark text have been sold in 20 languages around the globe.

"Nonviolent communication is a simple yet powerful methodology for communicating in a way that meets both parties' needs. This is one of the most useful books you will ever read."
—William Ury, co-author of *Getting to Yes* and author of *The Third Side*

"I believe the principles and techniques in this book can literally change the world, but more importantly, they can change the quality of your life with your spouse, your children, your neighbors, your coworkers, and everyone else you interact with."
—Jack Canfield, author, *Chicken Soup for the Soul*

Available from PDP, CNVC, all major bookstores, and Amazon.com
Distributed by IPG: 800-888-4741

Nonviolent Communication Companion Workbook

A Practical Guide for Individual, Group, or Classroom Study

by Lucy Leu

$19.95 — Trade Paper 7x10, 224pp, ISBN: 978-1-892005-04-5

Learning Nonviolent Communication has often been equated with learning a whole new language. *The NVC Companion Workbook* helps you put these powerful, effective skills into practice with chapter-by-chapter study of Rosenberg's cornerstone text, *NVC: A Language of Life*. Create a safe, supportive group learning or practice environment that nurtures the needs of each participant. Find a wealth of activities, exercises, and facilitator suggestions to refine and practice this powerful communication process.

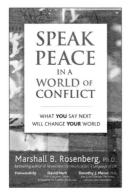

Speak Peace in a World of Conflict

What You Say Next Will Change Your World

by Marshall B. Rosenberg, Ph.D.

$15.95 — Trade Paper 5-3/8x8-3/8, 240pp, ISBN: 978-1-892005-17-5

International peacemaker, mediator, and healer, Rosenberg shows you how the language you use is the key to enriching life. *Speak Peace* is filled with inspiring stories, lessons, and ideas drawn from over 40 years of mediating conflicts and healing relationships in some of the most war-torn, impoverished, and violent corners of the world. Find insight, practical skills, and powerful tools that will profoundly change your relationships and the course of your life for the better.

Discover how you can create an internal consciousness of peace as the first step toward effective personal, professional, and social change. Find complete chapters on the mechanics of Speaking Peace, conflict resolution, transforming business culture, transforming enemy images, addressing terrorism, transforming authoritarian structures, expressing and receiving gratitude, and social change.

"*Speak Peace* is a book that comes at an appropriate time when anger and violence dominates human attitudes. Marshall Rosenberg gives us the means to create peace through our speech and communication. A brilliant book."

—Arun Gandhi, president, M. K. Gandhi Institute for Nonviolence, USA

Bestselling author of the internationally acclaimed, *Nonviolent Communication: A Language of Life*

Being Genuine

Stop Being Nice, Start Being Real

by Thomas d'Ansembourg

$15.95 — Trade Paper 5-3/8x8-3/8, 340pp, ISBN: 978-1-892005-21-2

Being Genuine brings Thomas d'Ansembourg's blockbuster French title to the English market. His work offers you a fresh new perspective on the proven skills offered in the bestselling book, *Nonviolent Communication: A Language of Life*. Drawing on his own real-life examples and stories, d'Ansembourg provides practical skills and concrete steps that allow us to safely remove the masks we wear, which prevent the intimacy and satisfaction we desire with our intimate partners, children, parents, friends, family, and colleagues.

"Through this book, we can feel Nonviolent Communication not as a formula but as a rich, meaningful way of life, both intellectually and emotionally."

—Vicki Robin, cofounder, Conversation Cafes, coauthor, *Your Money or Your Life*

Based on Marshall Rosenberg's Nonviolent Communication process

Available from PDP, CNVC, all major bookstores, and Amazon.com
Distributed by IPG: 800-888-4741

About the Authors

Sura Hart and **Victoria Kindle Hodson** are coauthors of *The No-Fault Classroom* and *Respectful Parents, Respectful Kids: 7 Keys to Turn Family Conflict into Co-operation.* They bring to their work a combined forty-five years of teaching young people as well as teachers, administrators and parents in school communities. As co-founders of Kindle-Hart Communication.™ Sura and Victoria have been developing and facilitating parent- and teacher-education workshops together for more than twenty years.

Sura Hart is an internationally recognized CNVC certified Nonviolent Communication (NVC) trainer known as a worldwide leader in the incorporation of the NVC process in schools. She designs and facilitates trainings for students, parents, teachers and school administrators around the globe. She has been a classroom teacher and has worked with at-risk youth, creating and delivering programs on leadership, effective communication, healthy sexuality and conflict resolution. Sura serves as the contact person for CNVC's efforts to integrate NVC in U.S. schools.

Victoria Kindle Hodson, MA, holds degrees in education and psychology and has been a classroom teacher in public and private schools. She is the co-director of the LearningSuccess Institute in Ventura, California, where teachers, school administrators, therapists and parents train in coaching skills and is the coauthor, with Mariaemma Willis, of the best-selling book *Discover Your Child's Learning Style.* Victoria is currently conducting initiatives to implement Nonviolent Communication and LearningSuccess principles and practices in charter schools in the United States and Canada.

Sura lives in Seattle, Washington, and Victoria lives in Southern California.

For a schedule of their upcoming serminars for school administrators, staff, teachers and parents or to order their No-Fault Game and books, please visit **www.k-hcommunication.com**